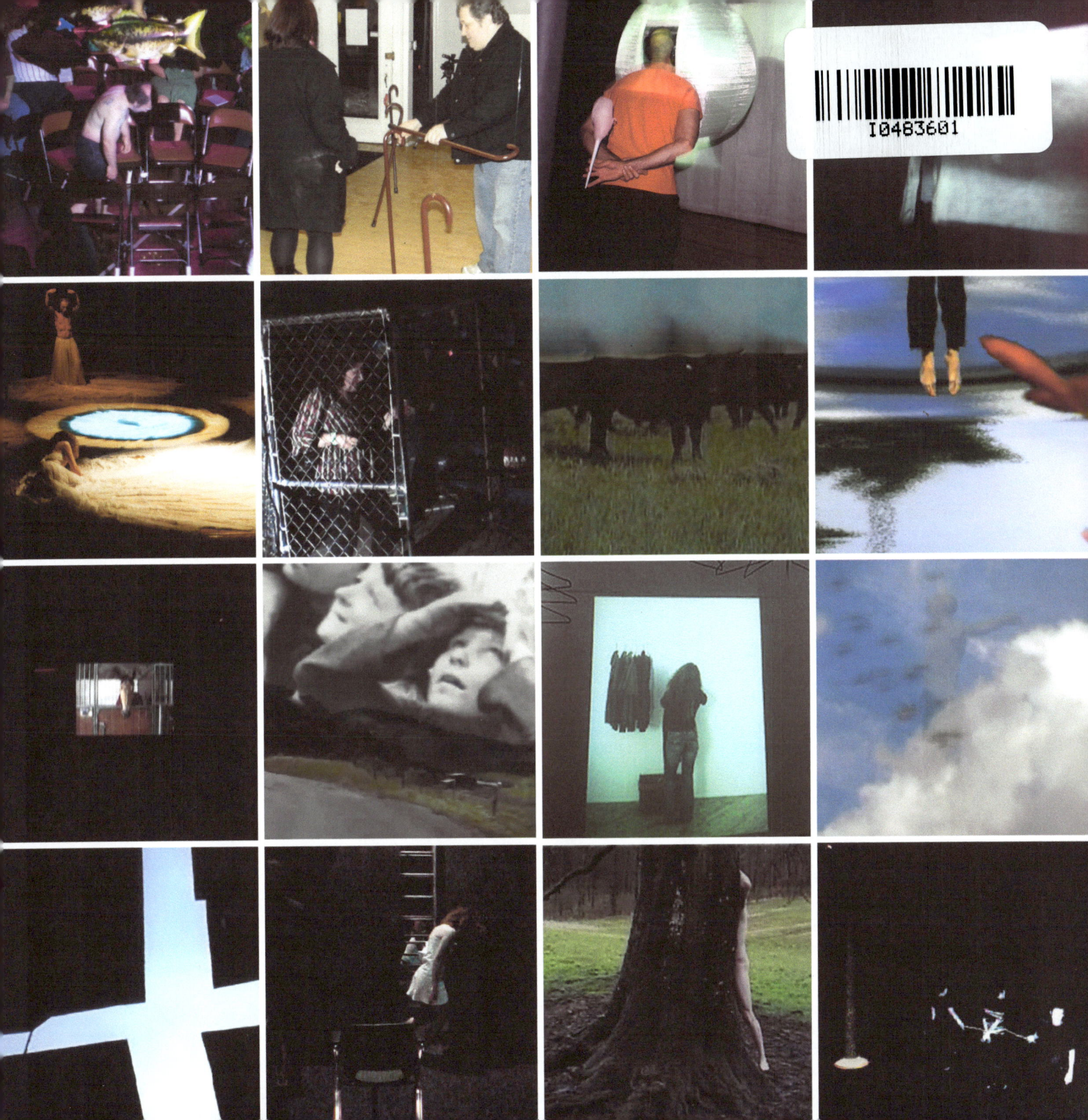

ScenoArt
293 Linwood Ave
Buffalo, NY 14209
www.scenoart.net
info@scenoart.net

First ScenoArt Edition 2014

Book layout design / Cover artwork by Ella Joseph
Printed in the United States of America by Lightning Source

ISBN 978-0-9845319-2-9

Ella Joseph is a visual and theatre performance artist. Born in Iasi, Romania, she left her country in 1995 to freely pursue her dream of becoming an artist. Ella trained in visual and physical performance at the Utrecht School of the Arts (HKU), The Netherlands; video, photography and public art at the School of Art and Design Zurich (HGKZ), Switzerland; and painting at the George Enescu University of Arts, Iasi, Romania. She holds a Master of Arts in scenography from Central Saint Martins School of Art & Design, United Kingdom, a Master of Fine Arts in theatre design from the University of British Columbia, Vancouver, Canada, and a Master of Science in textile design from the Gh. Asachi Technical University of Iasi, Romania. In 2004 she founded *ScenoArt*, "the art of writing in space," with the mission to create works at the intersections of visual and performing arts, where theatre, performance, art installations and fine-art exhibitions cohabit and influence each other; and titled her works and writing series on the process of creation under the collective name *Theatre of Truth(s)*. Consisting of over twenty-five original pieces, Ella's work has been shown in Europe, Canada and the United States.

To my Father

Catalogue of Works

Theatre of Truth(s) Series

Contents

Theatre of Truth(s)

10

Introduction

Have you ever had difficulties explaining what you do? When you make art, people often ask what kind of art you make. If you are not a painter or a sculptor or you can't define what you do by one simple word, be ready to encounter disappointed, confused, sometimes dismissive faces: obviously, your response was not what your audience expected to hear.

One day, I was having a cup of coffee at my studio with a fellow artist who has been following my work for a number of years. He confessed that he still could not fathom if my work belonged into the realm of visual arts or into the realm of theatre. I answered yes; my work stands at the intersection of visual and performing arts. At this juncture, I get to pick and choose, bend and blend, elements of both, veiling and unveiling my own truth. To see if he could better understand my vision, I showed him more images of my work. After a while, he exclaimed: *I think I finally got it!*

Theatre of Truth(s) catalogue brings together sixteen works and makes a fine companion to the Theatre of Truth(s) book series which carries the intent to reveal my process of creation, one work at a time. Far from pretending to (un)cover all facets of my art making, this minimal collection of images, which culminates with a collage of written statements from my viewers, peals back another layer in the artwork. Besides, for the sake of art and entertainment, the format of the catalogue lends itself to make a great coffee table book for you to enjoy!

12

Jonah Interrupted

Theatre Performance. Site Specific.

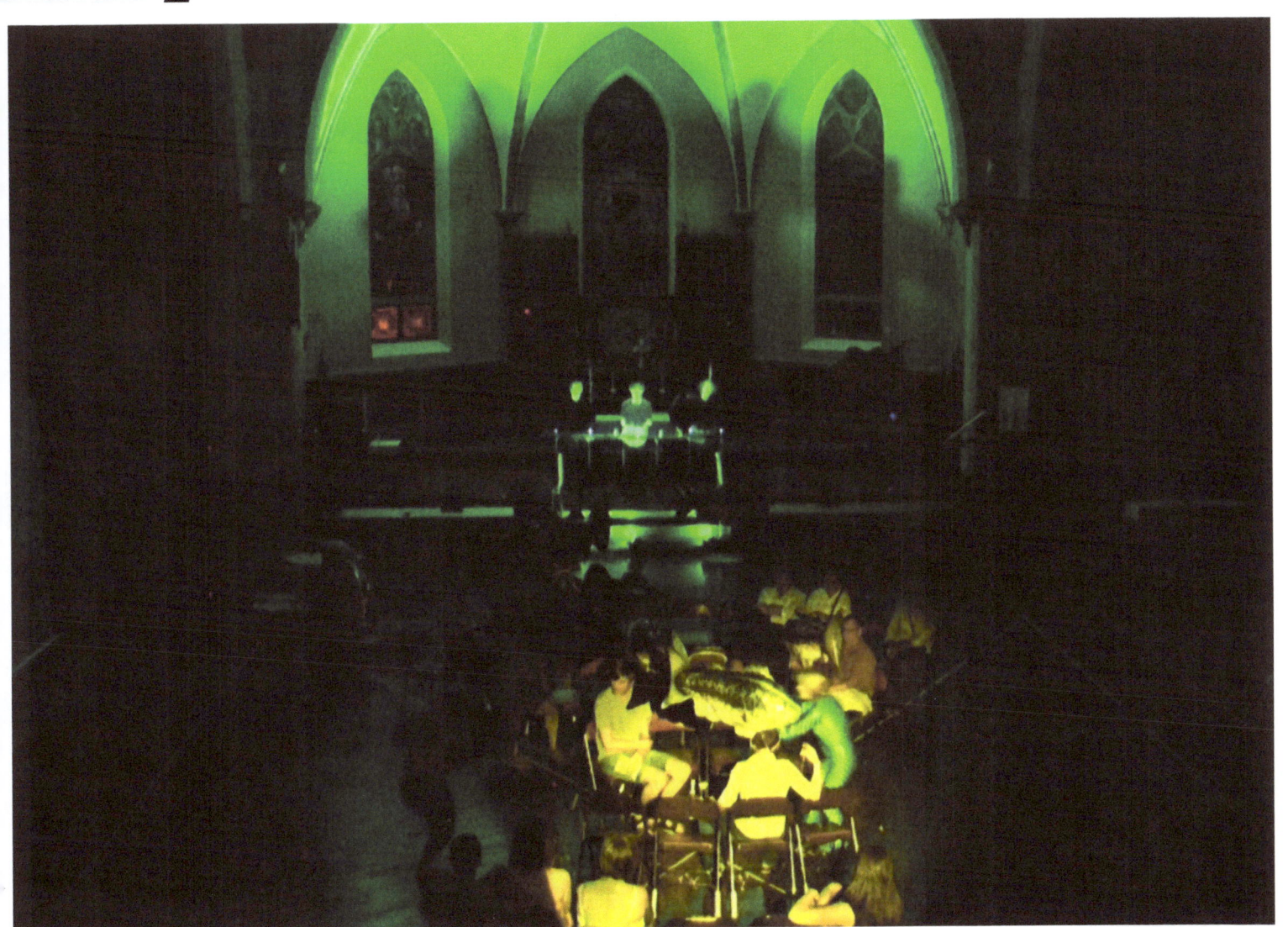

Jonah Interrupted

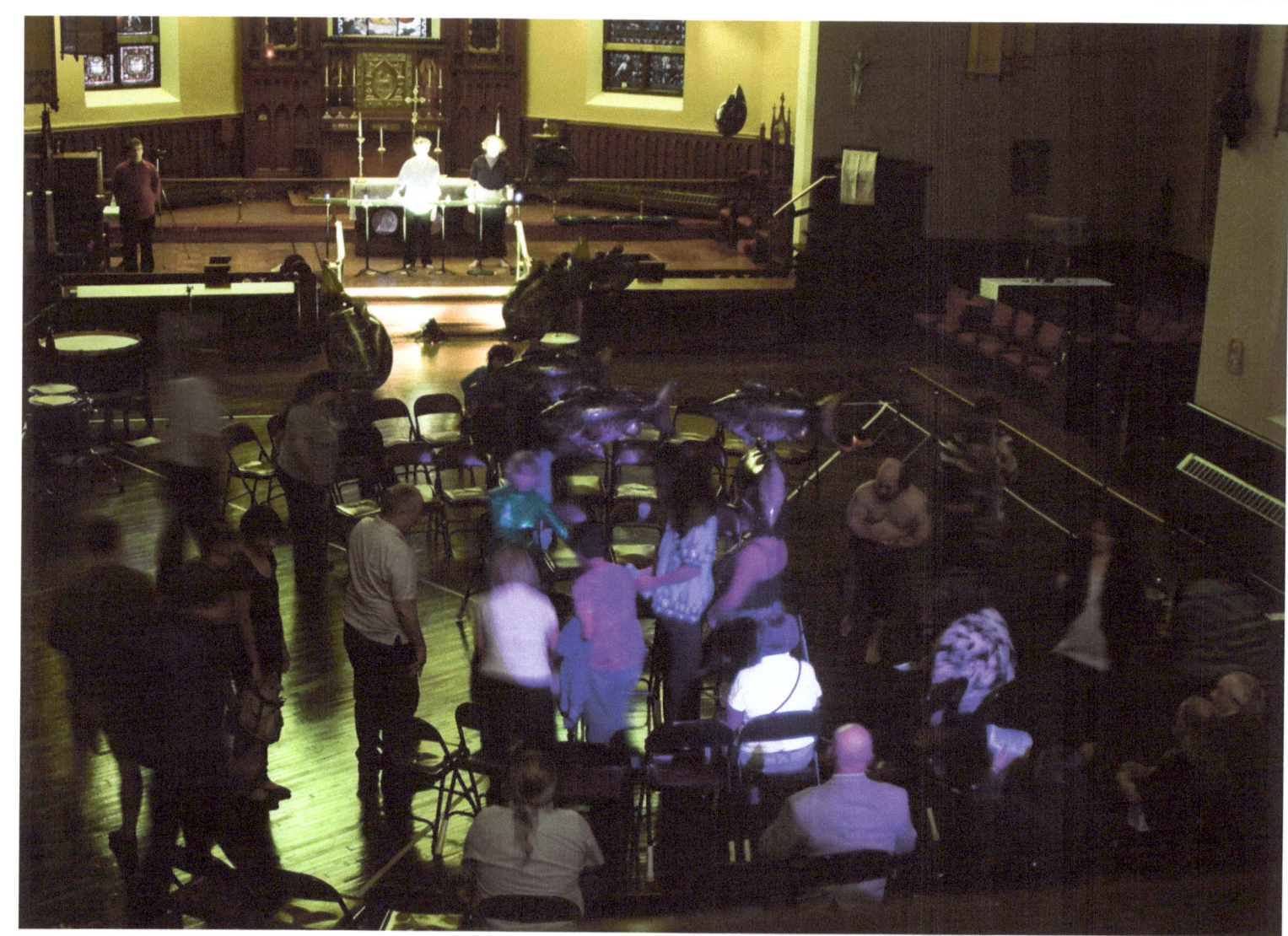

Theatre of Truth(s)

14

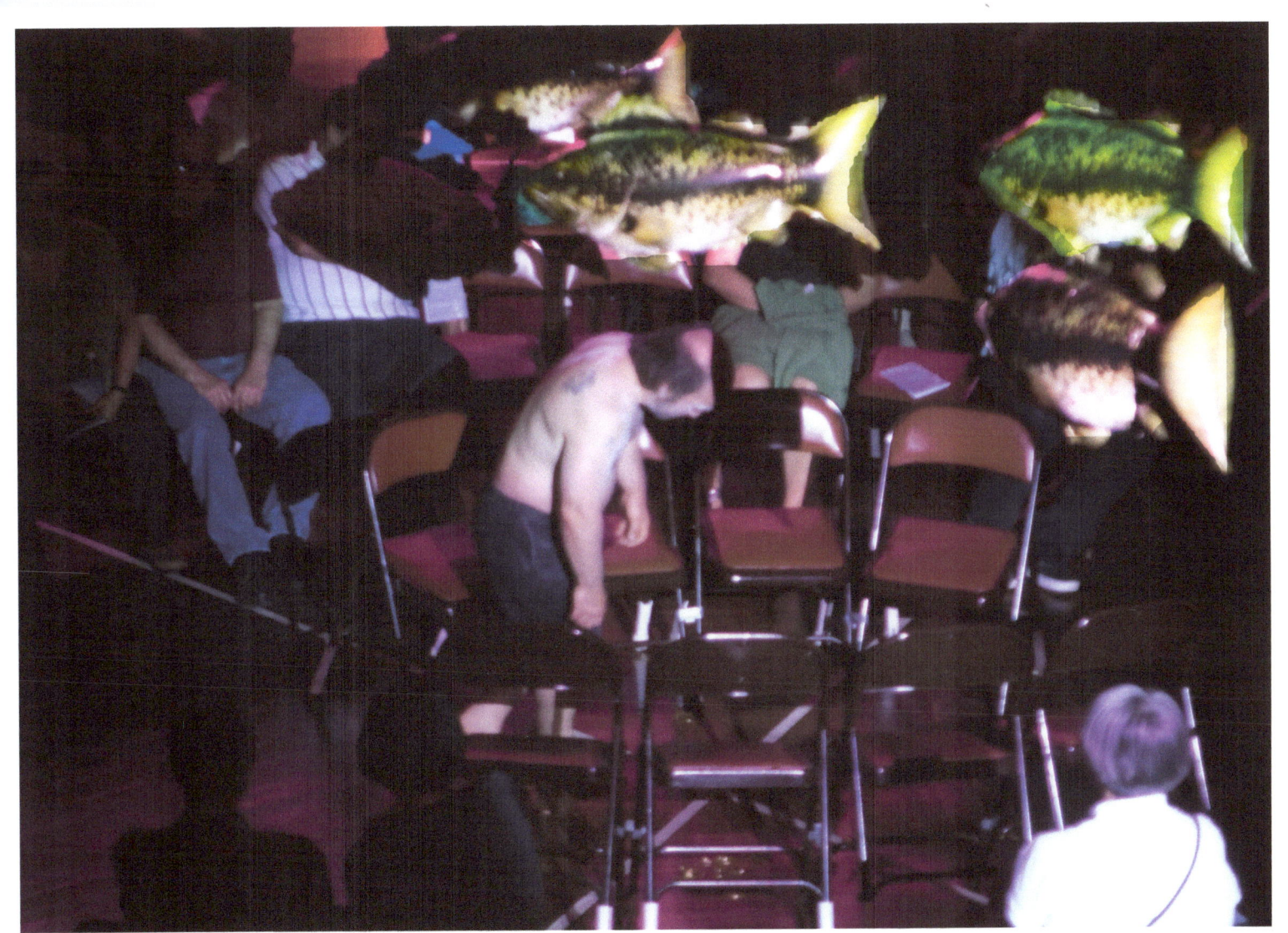

Jonah Interrupted

15

16

Awaiting Your Arrival

Performance-based Installation and Video. Site Specific.

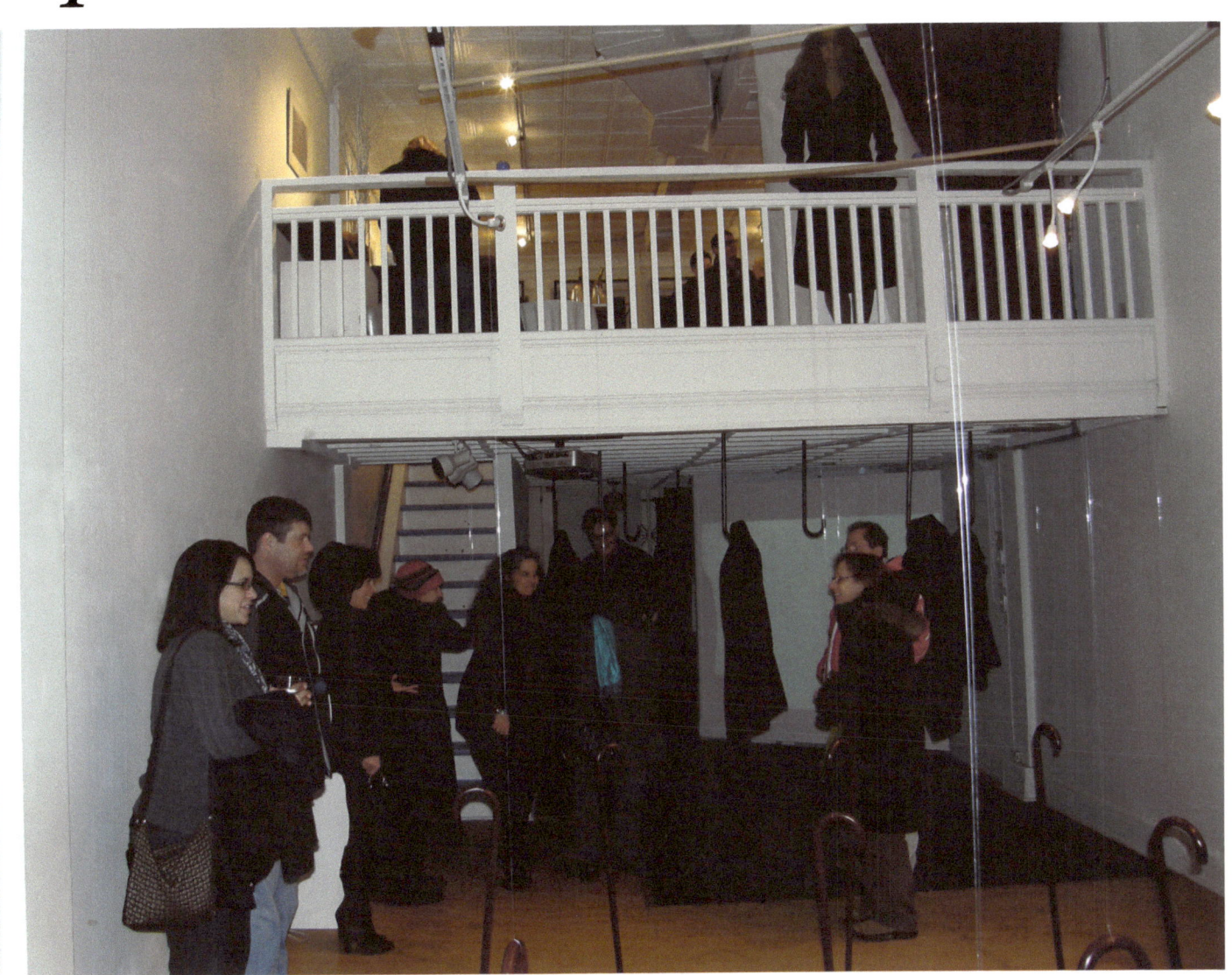

Awaiting Your Arrival

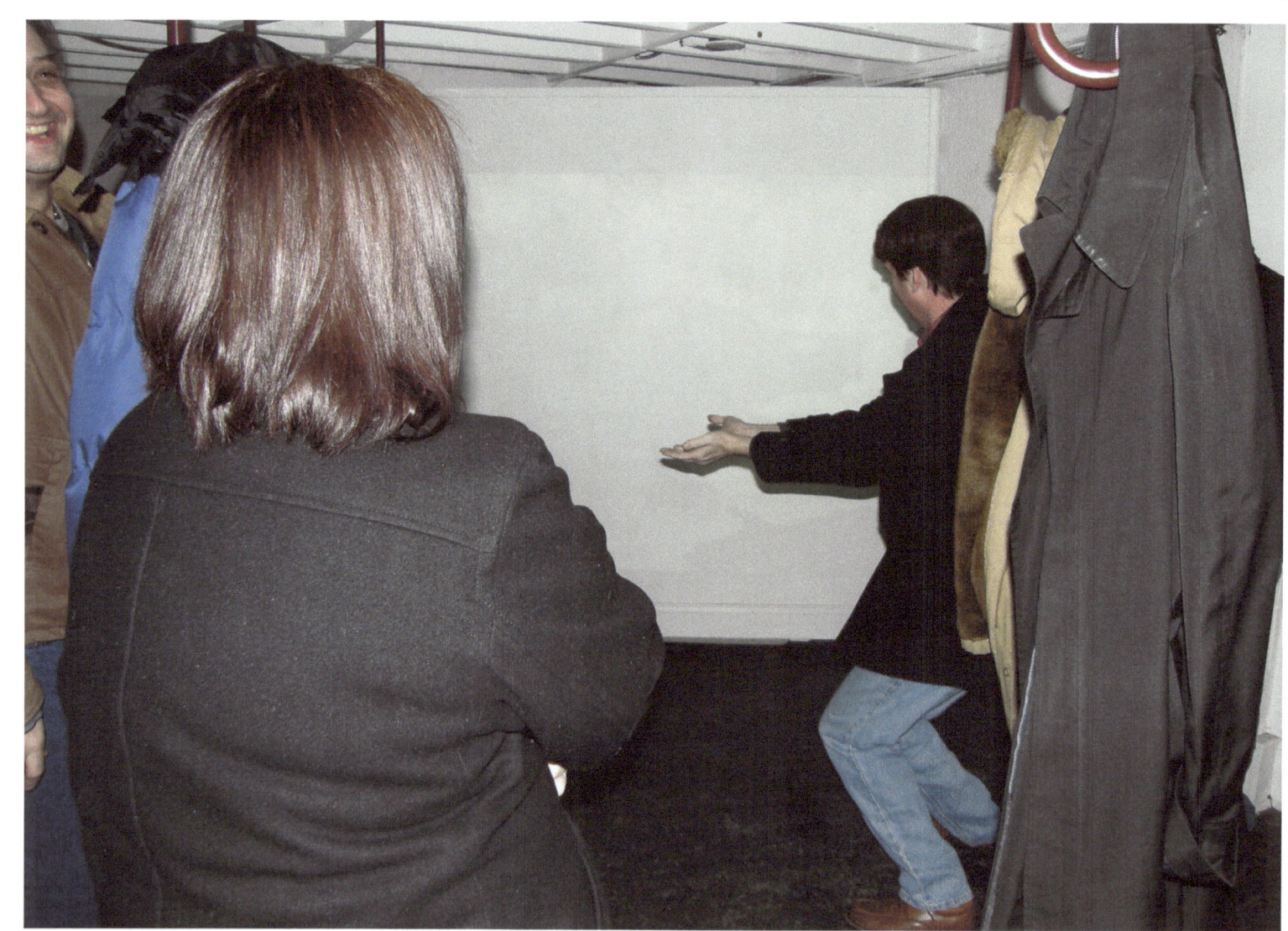

Theatre of Truth(s)

18

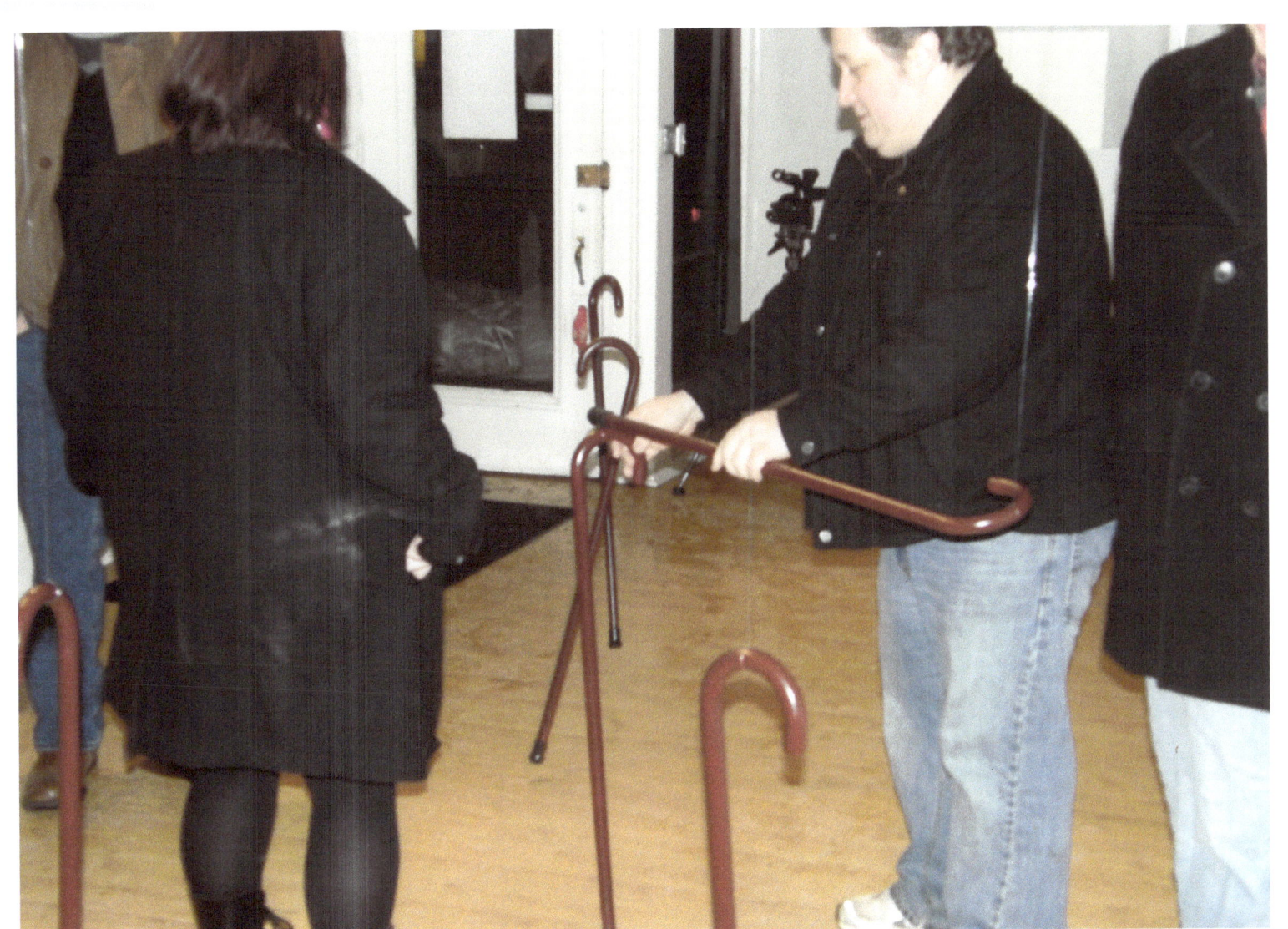

Awaiting Your Arrival

19

Theatre of Truth(s)

Cotton Candy...Cawcawphobia

Performance-based Installation with Sound and Video.

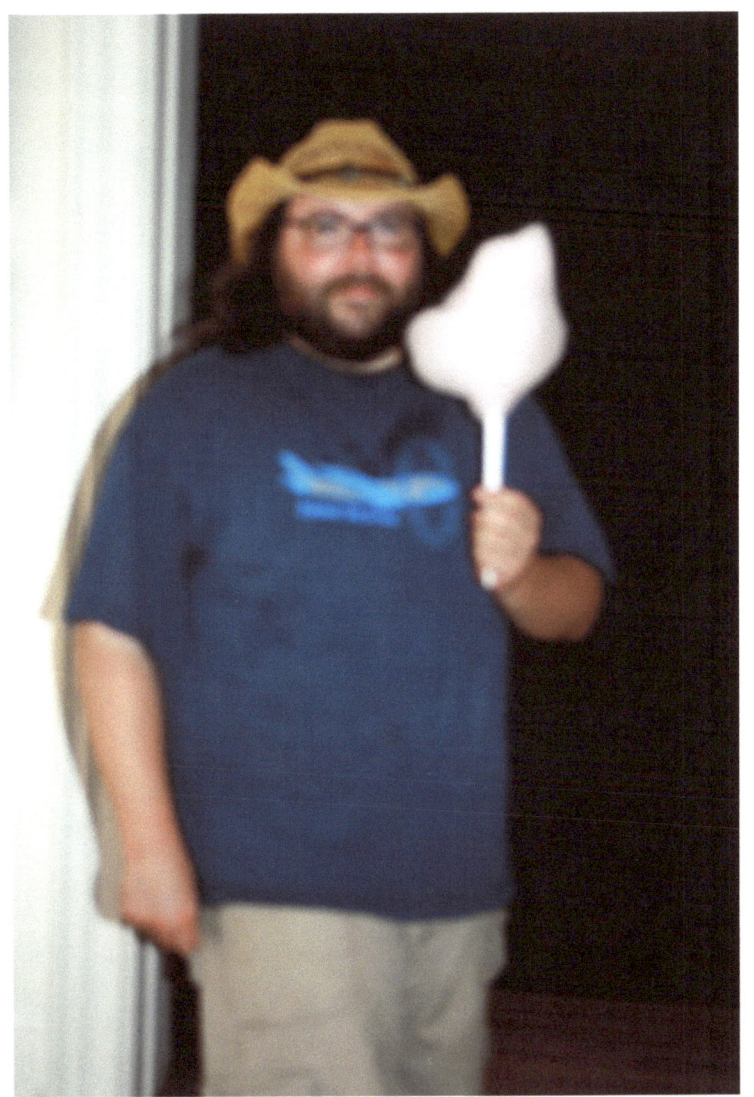

Cotton Candy...Cawcawphobia

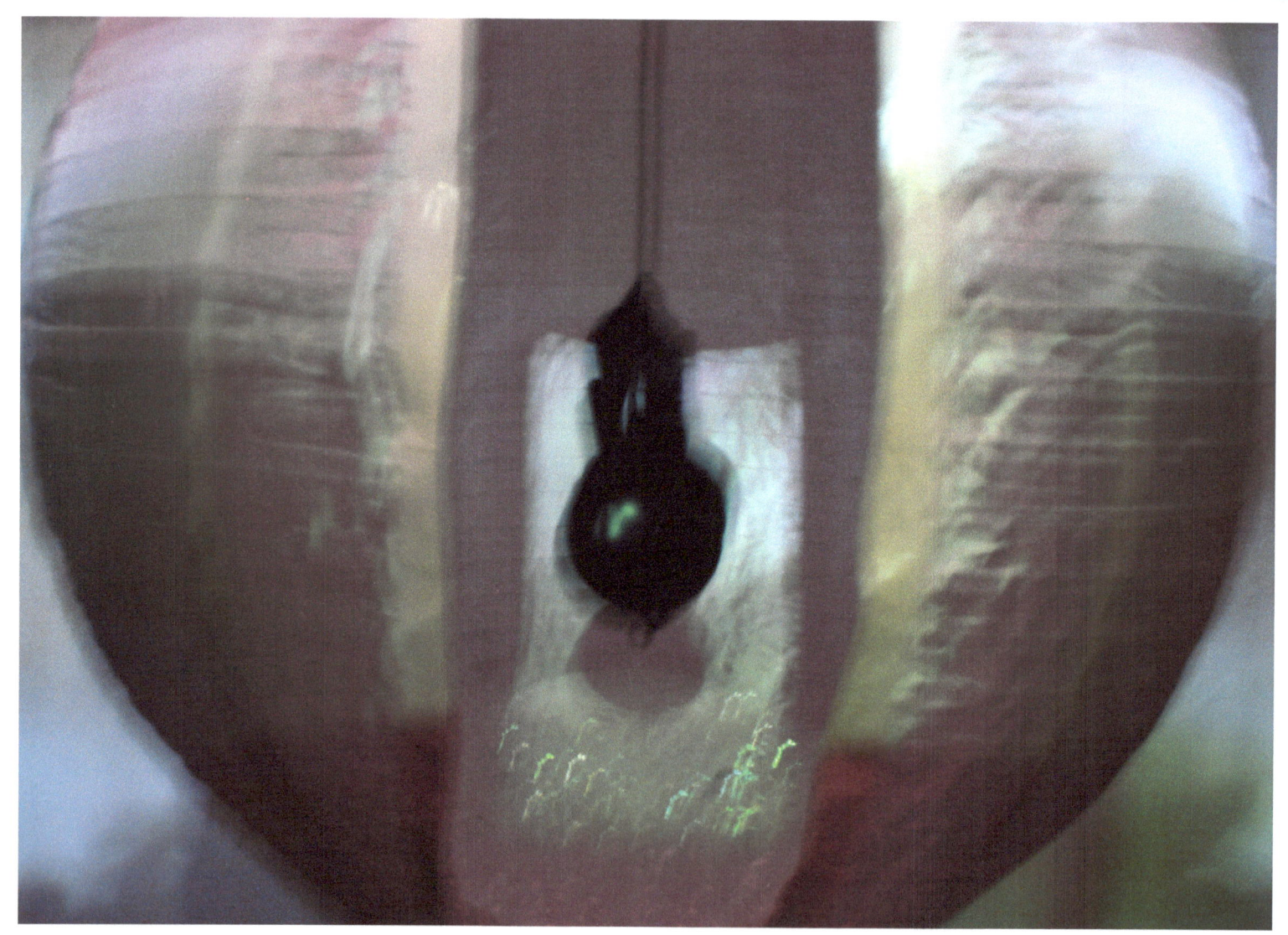

Theatre of Truth(s)

22

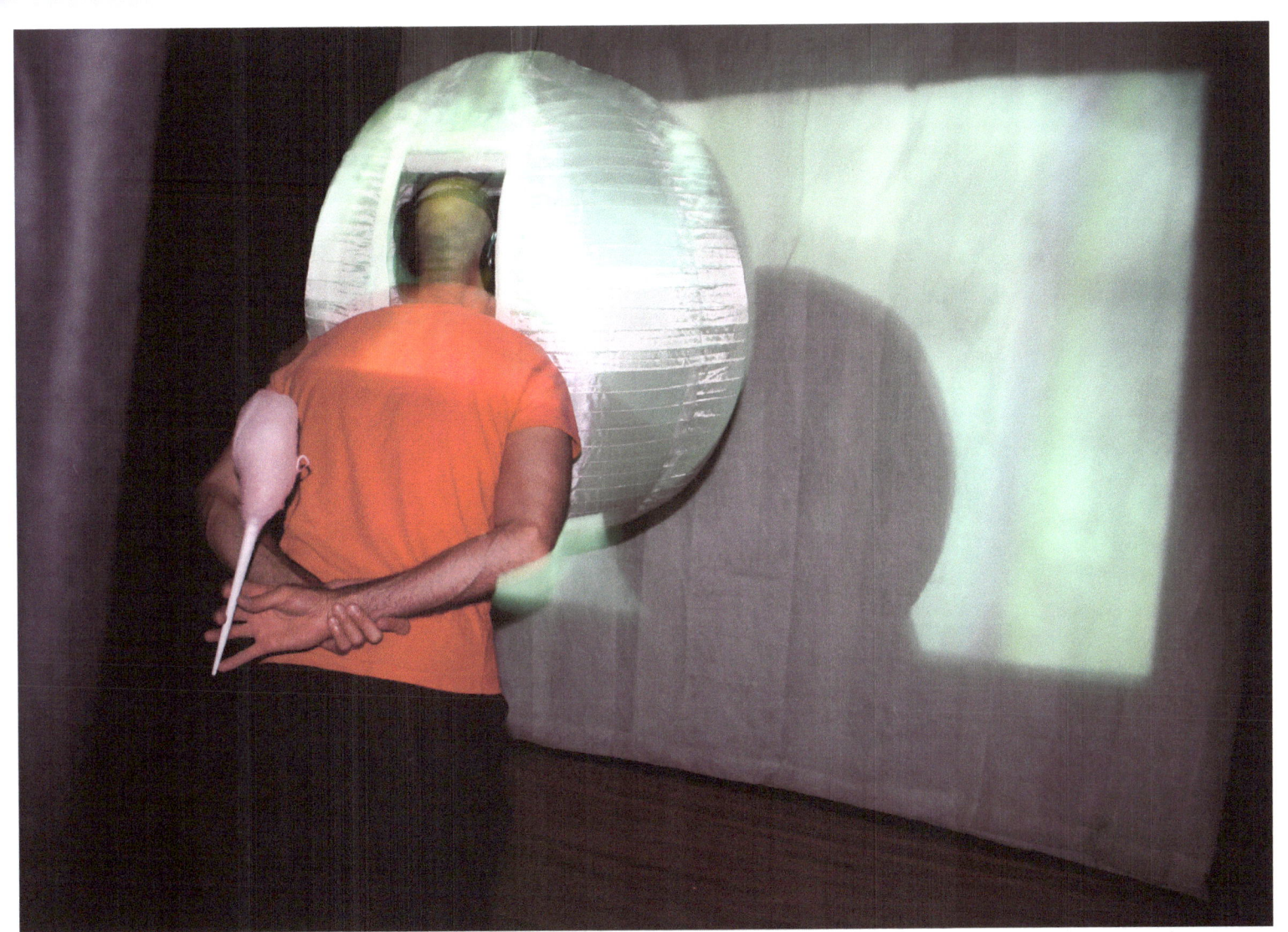

Cotton Candy...Cawcawphobia

23

24

A House of Stone
or Sunk In

*P*erformance-based Video Installation.

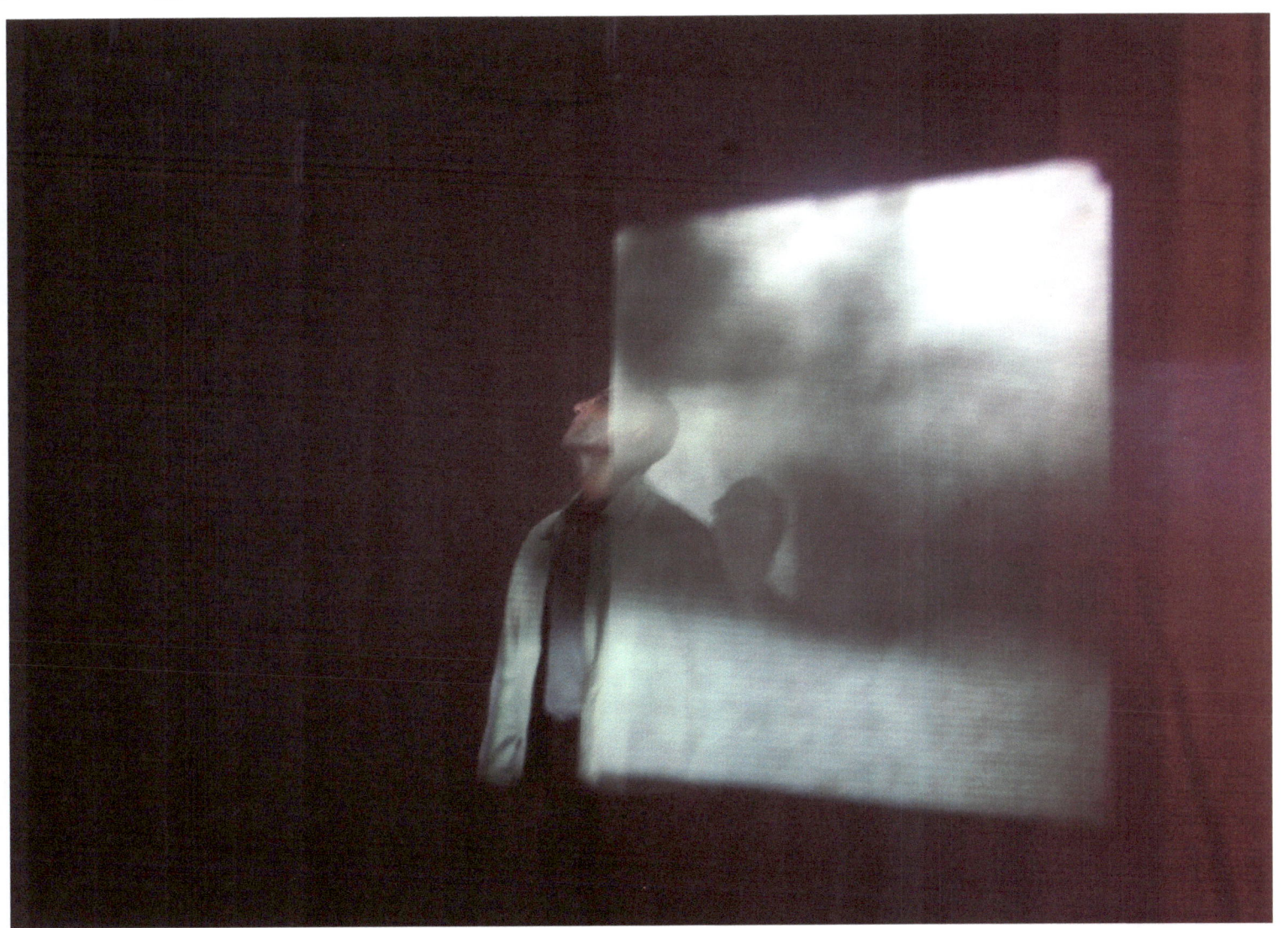

A House of Stone or Sunk In

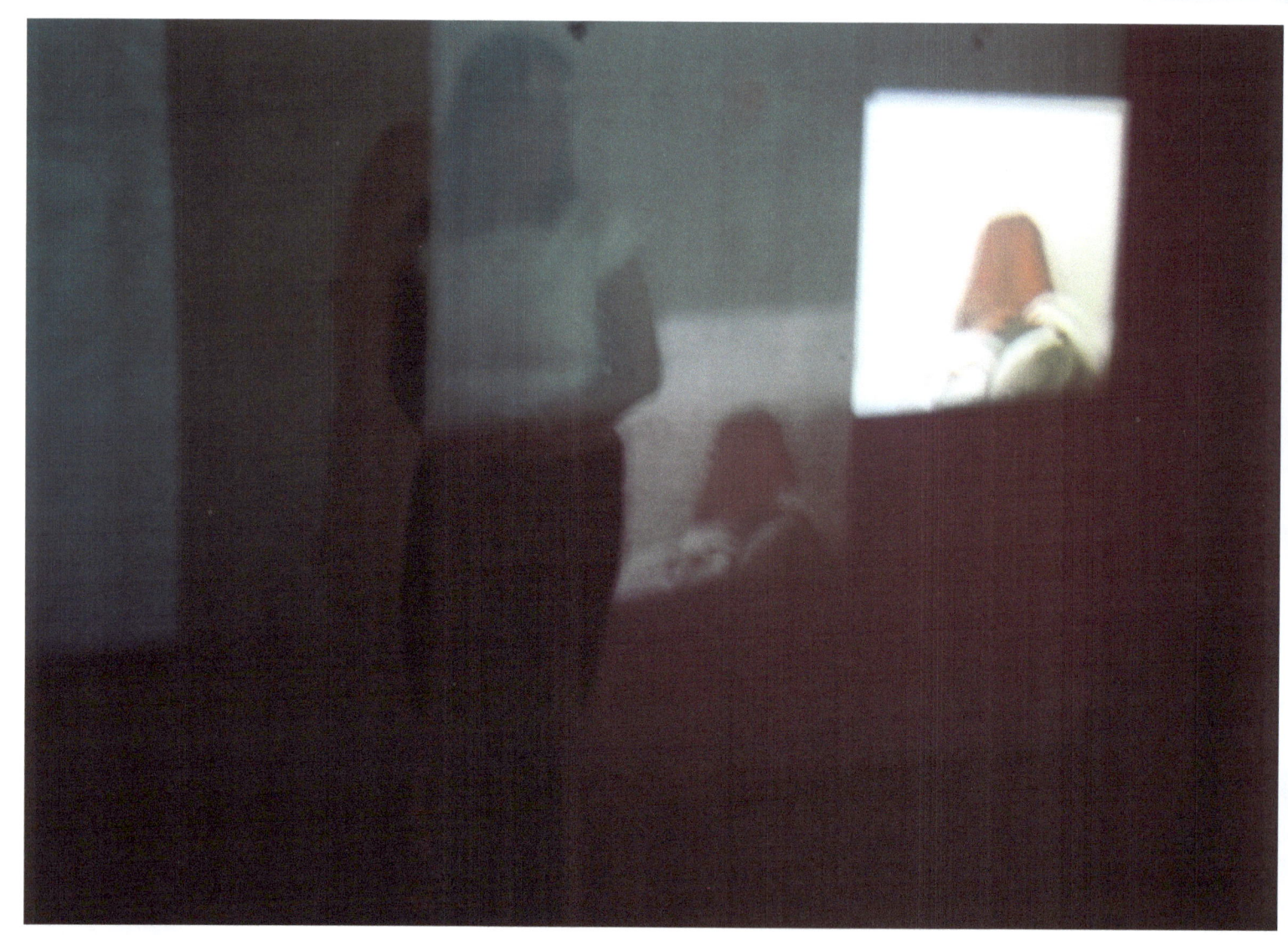

Theatre of Truth(s)

26

Video Still. Art Print.

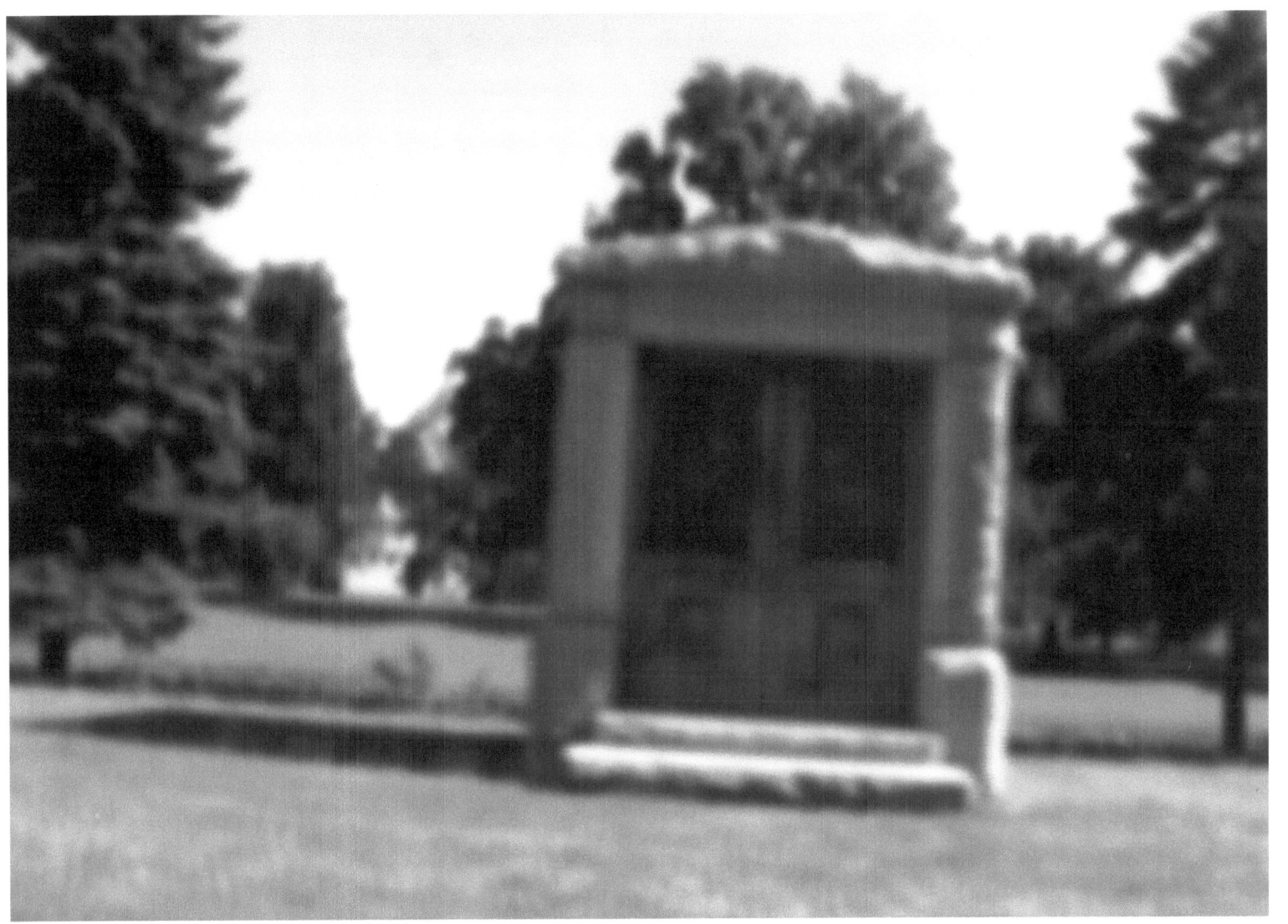

A House of Stone or Sunk In

27

28

Parsifal Unspoken

Performance of Movement, Sound and Video Projections. Site Specific.

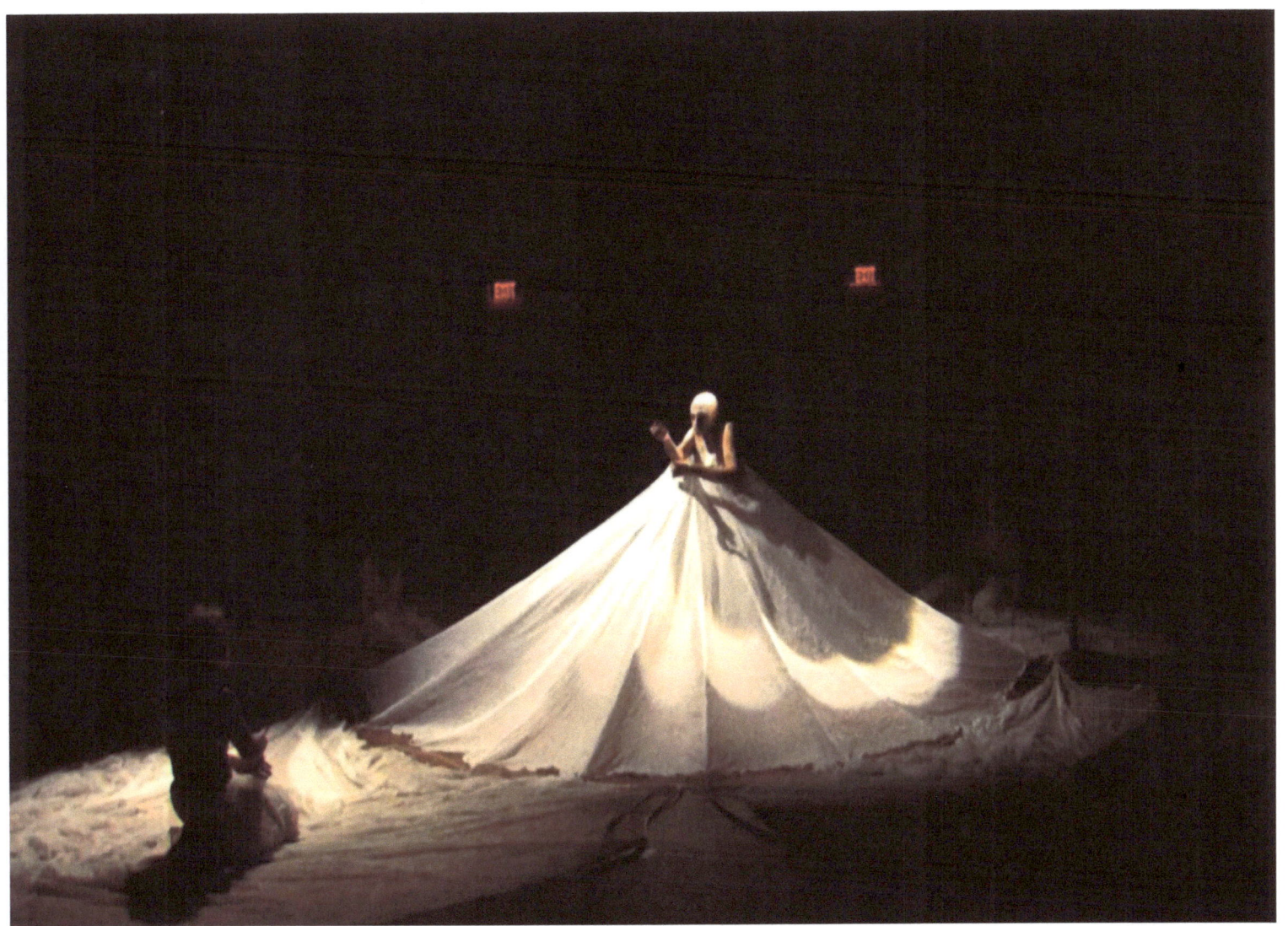

Parsifal Unspoken

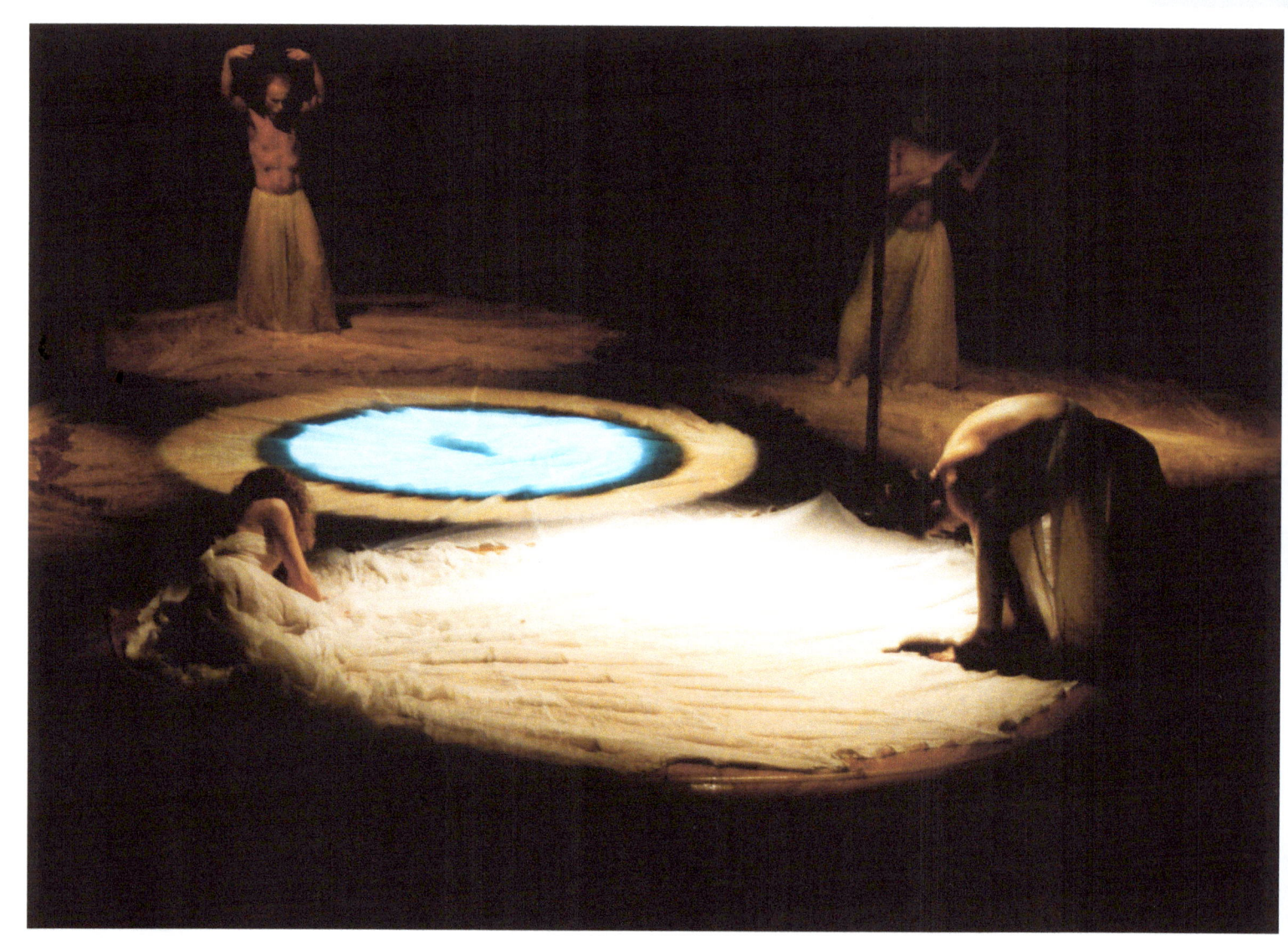

Theatre of Truth(s)

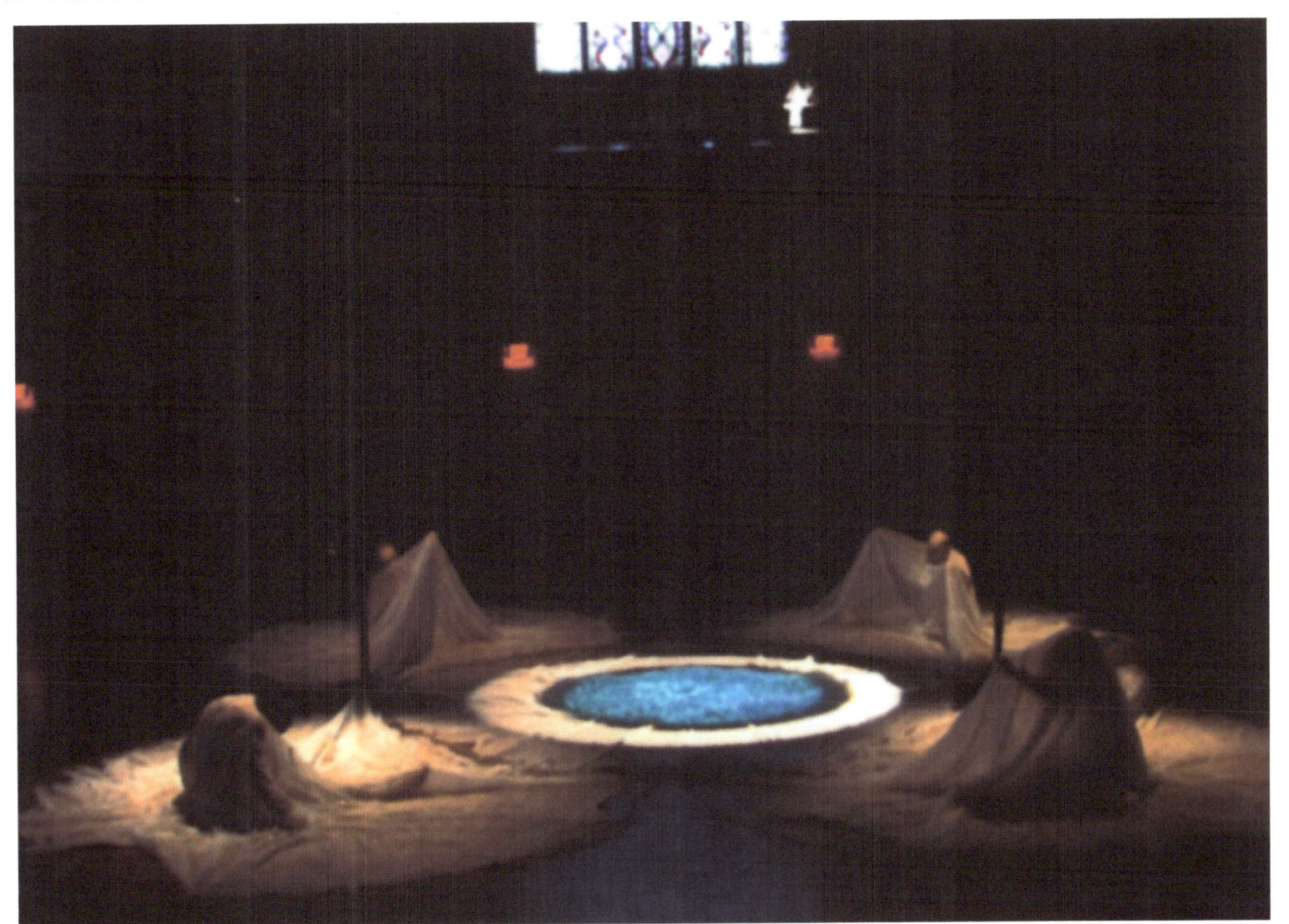

Parsifal Unspoken

31

32

All Aboard

Performance-based Installation with Video and Sound. Site Specific.

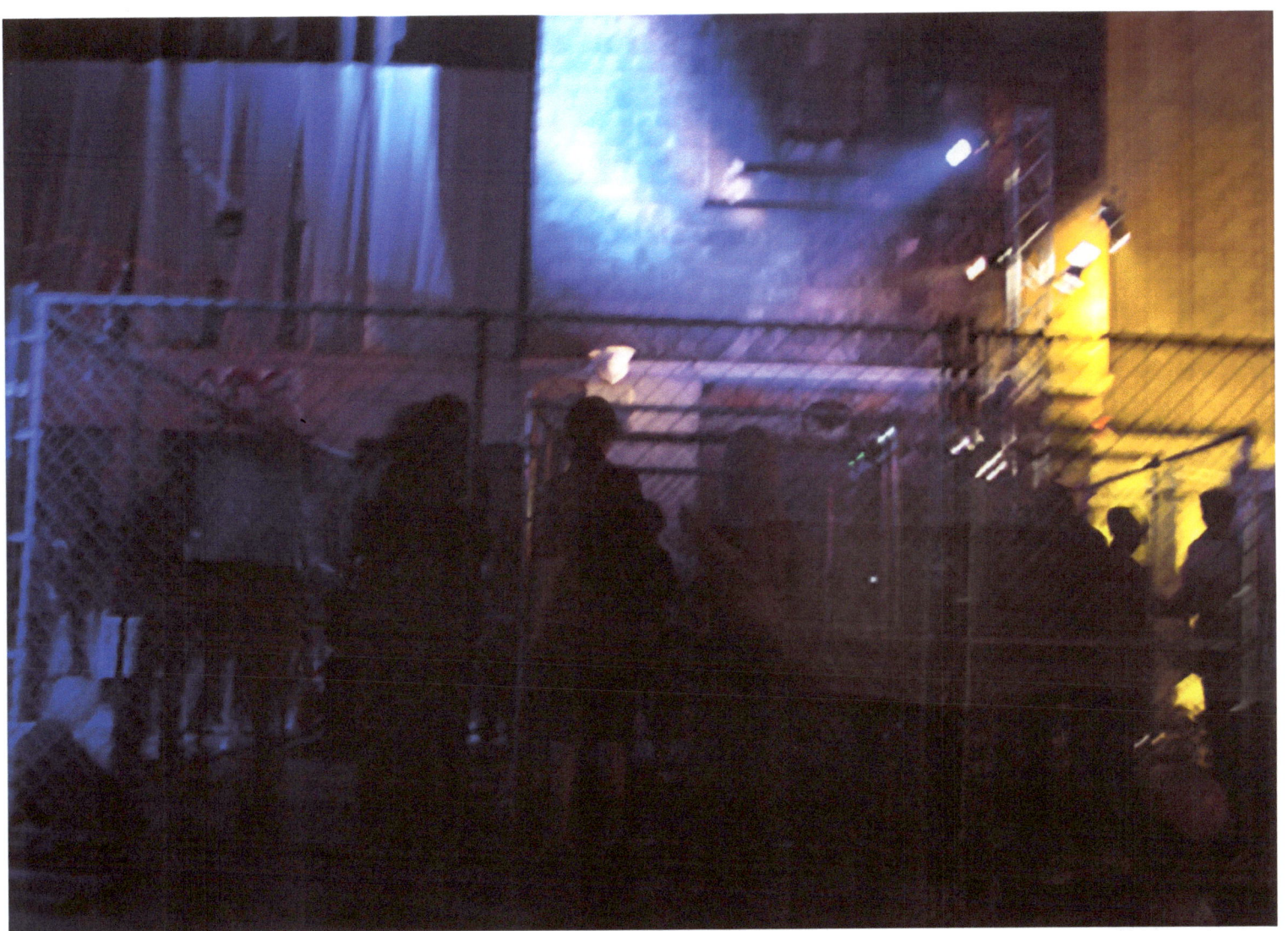

All Aboard

33

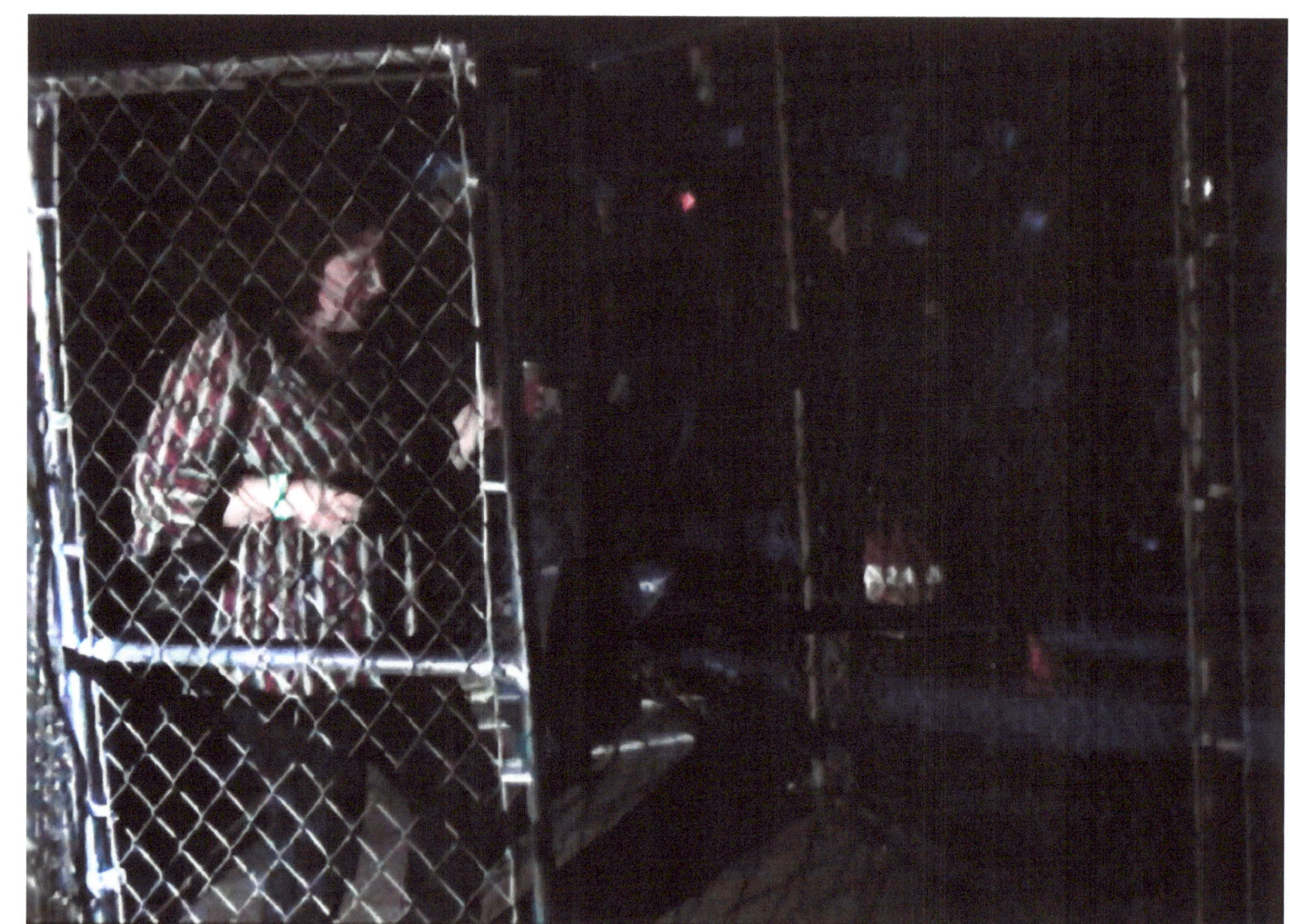

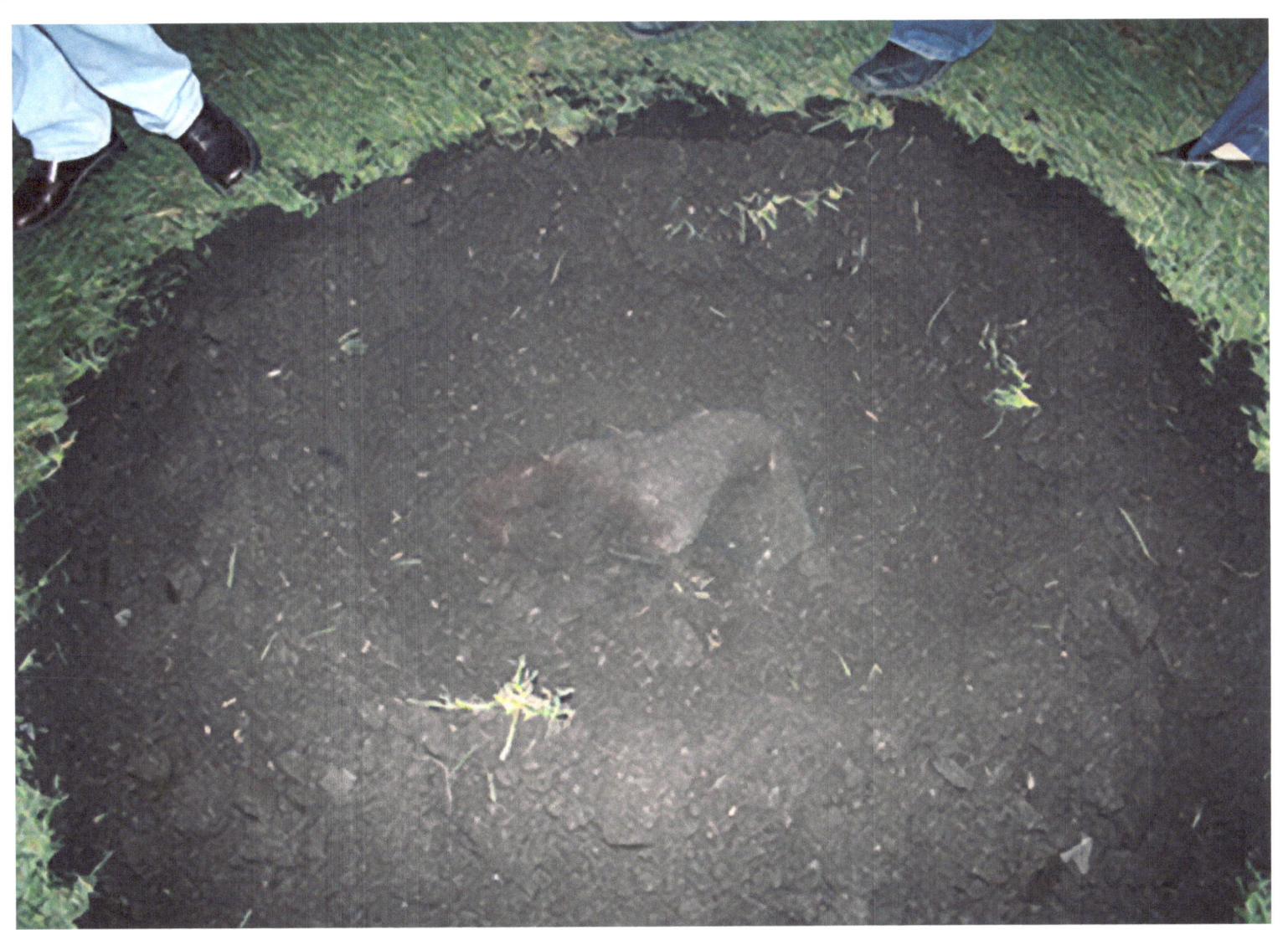

All Aboard

35

Theatre of Truth(s)

A Piece of Earth
or Shake Yourself Free

*V*ideo Installation.

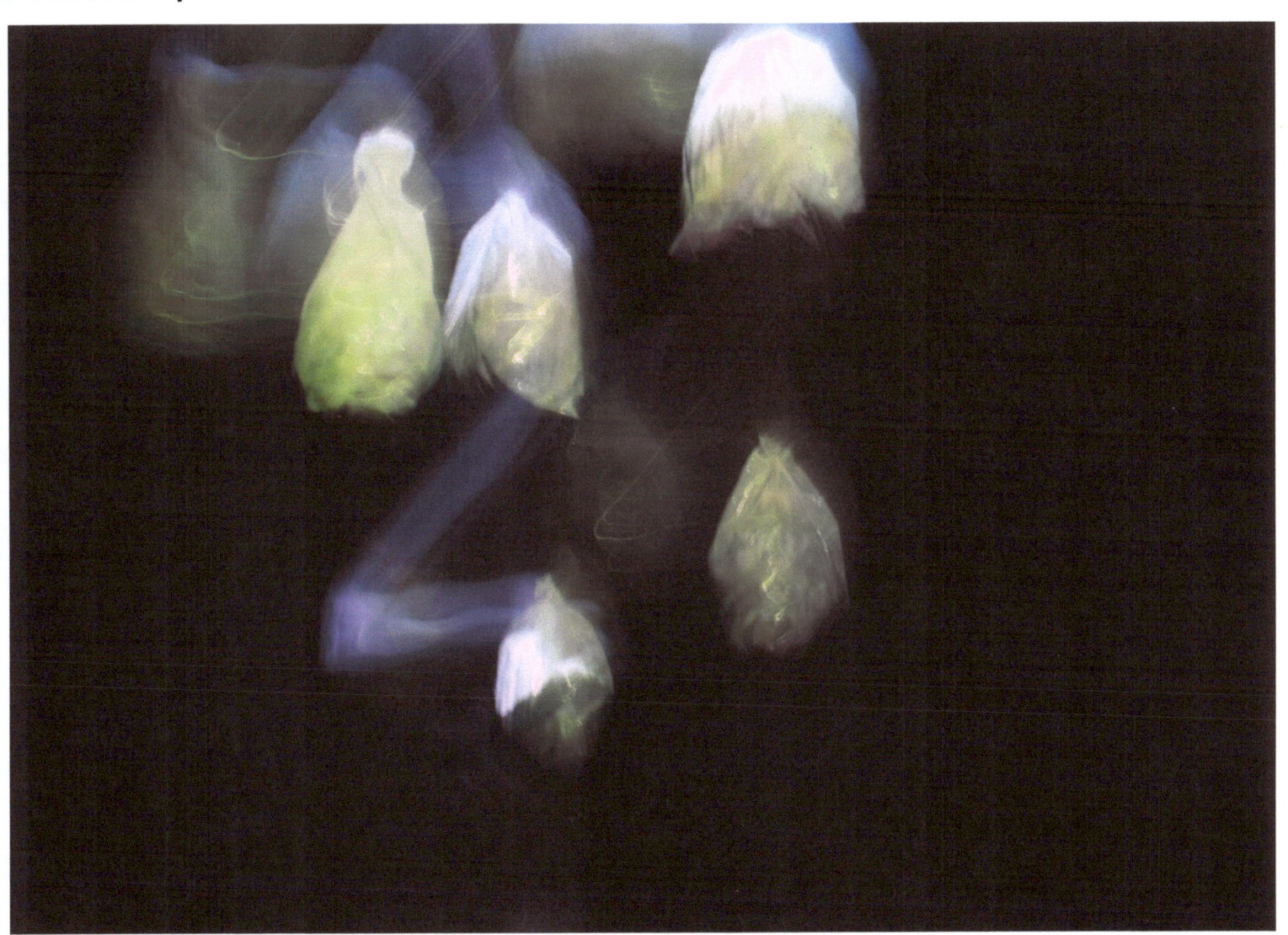

A Piece of Earth or Shake Yourself Free

37

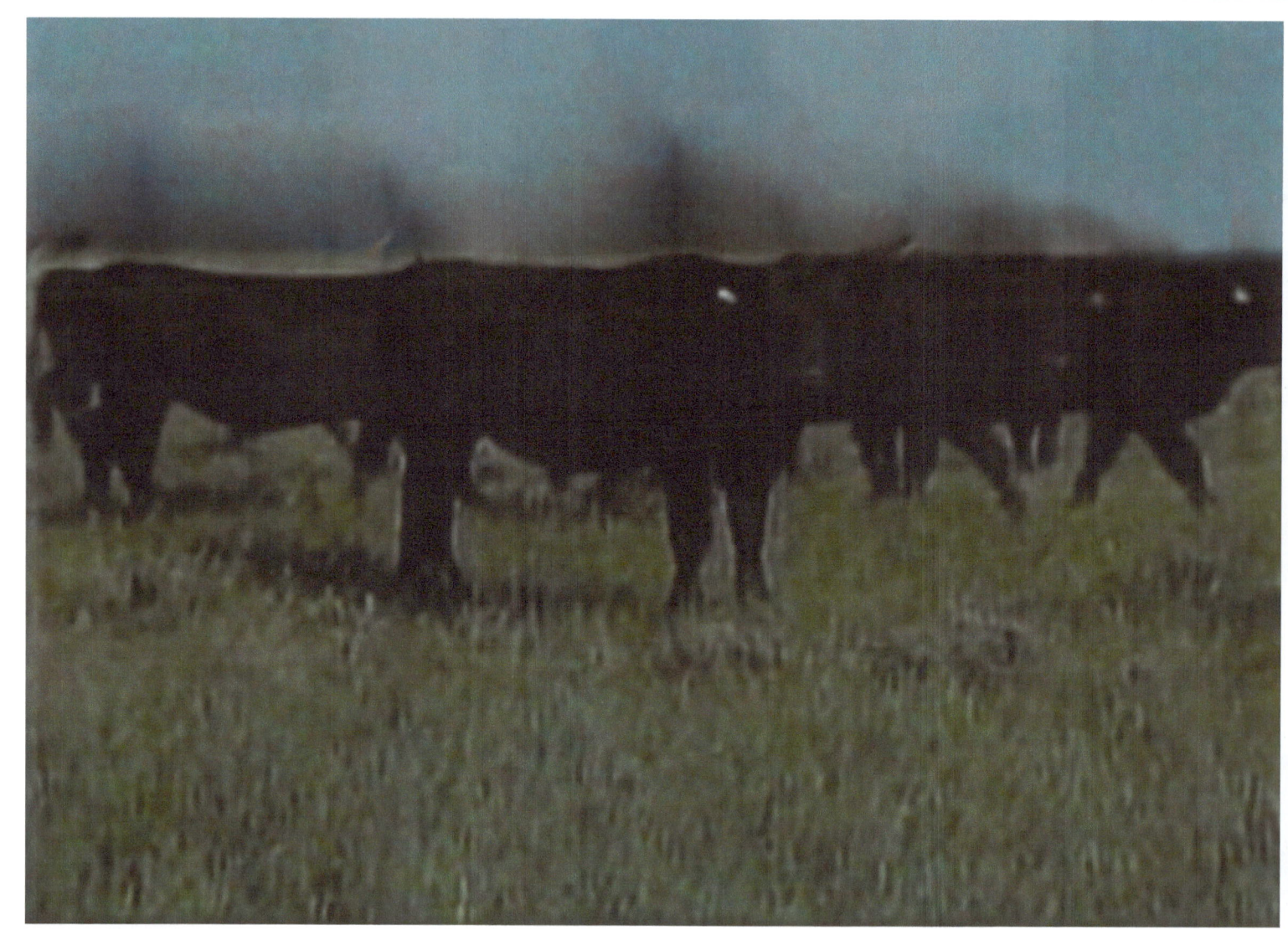

Theatre of Truth(s)

38

Video Stills. Art Prints.

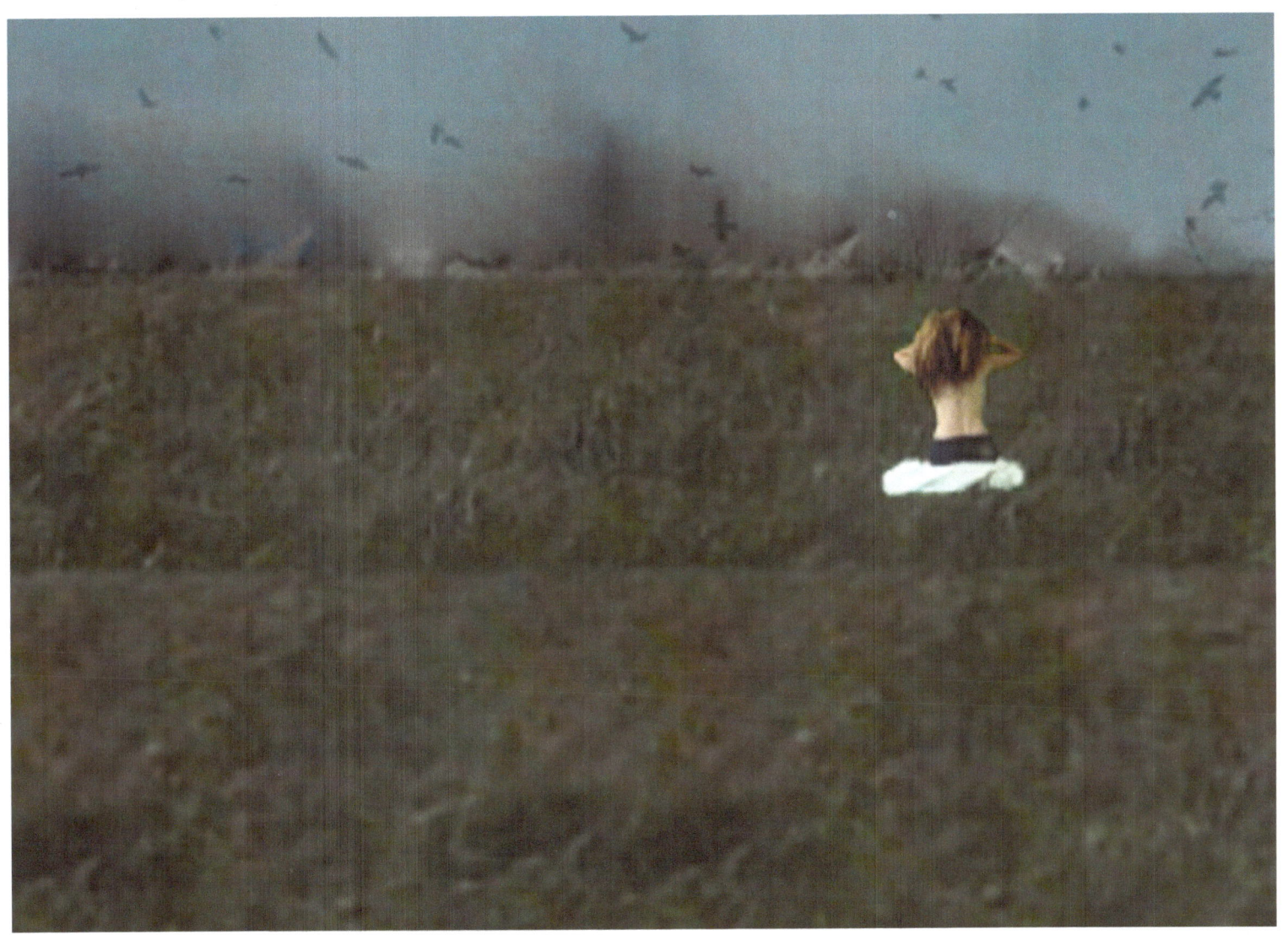

A Piece of Earth or Shake Yourself Free

39

Theatre of Truth(s)

40

Within Boundary
or A Ride in The Air

Installation with Video and Sound.

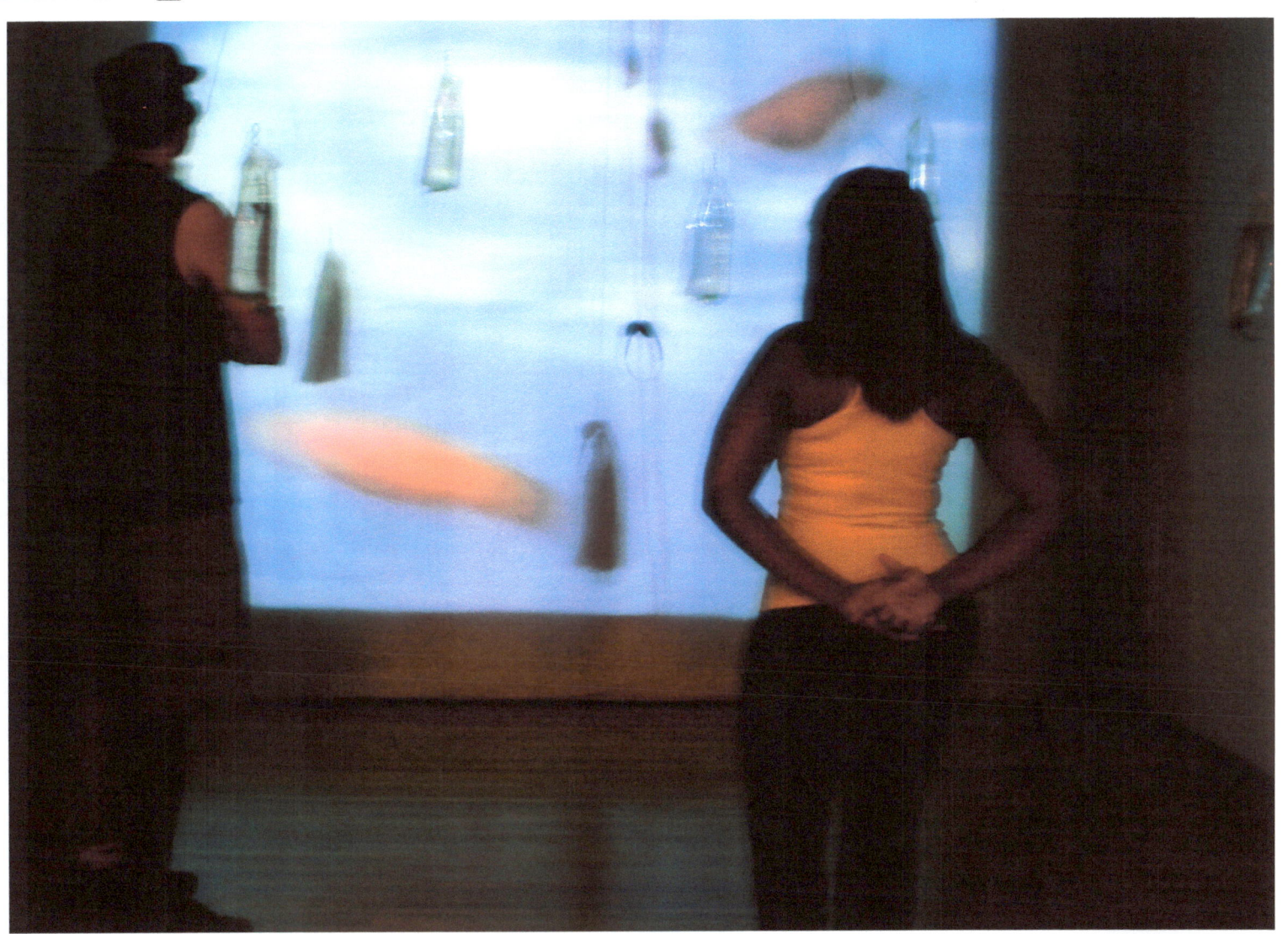

Within Boundary or A Ride in The Air

41

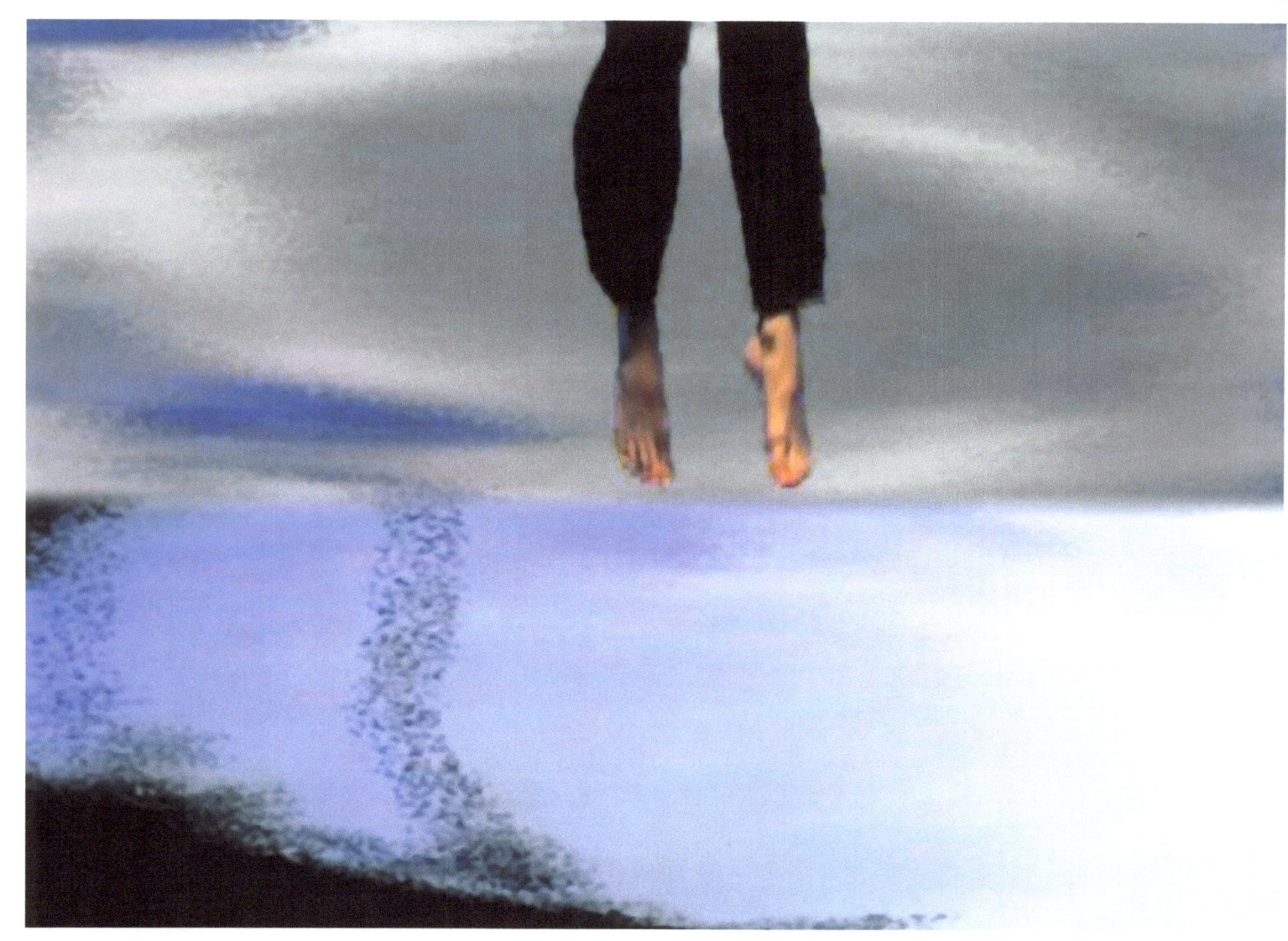

Theatre of Truth(s)

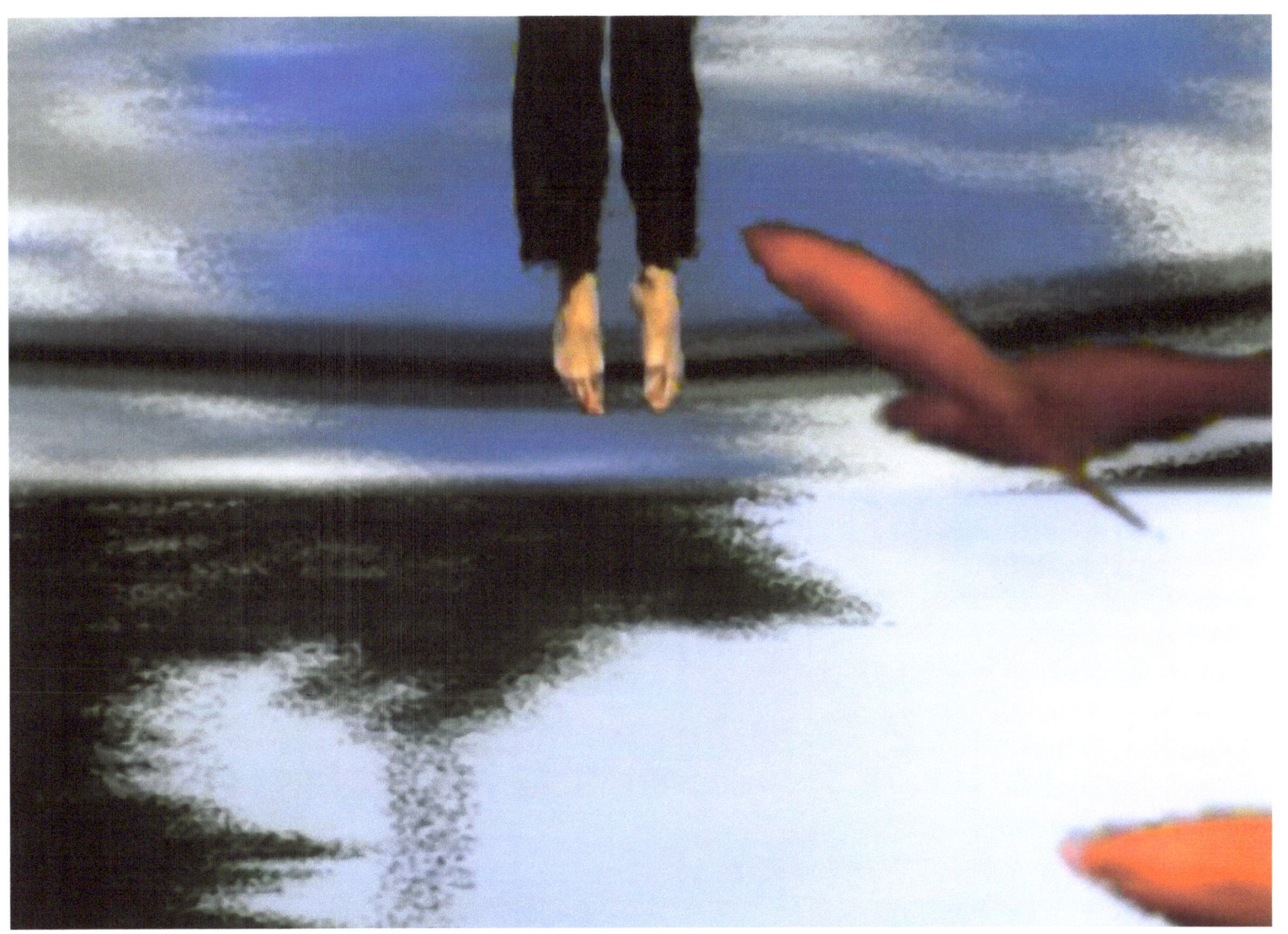

Within Boundary or A Ride in The Air

43

44

Over the Rainbow...Somewhere

*V*ideo. Video Stills. Art Prints.

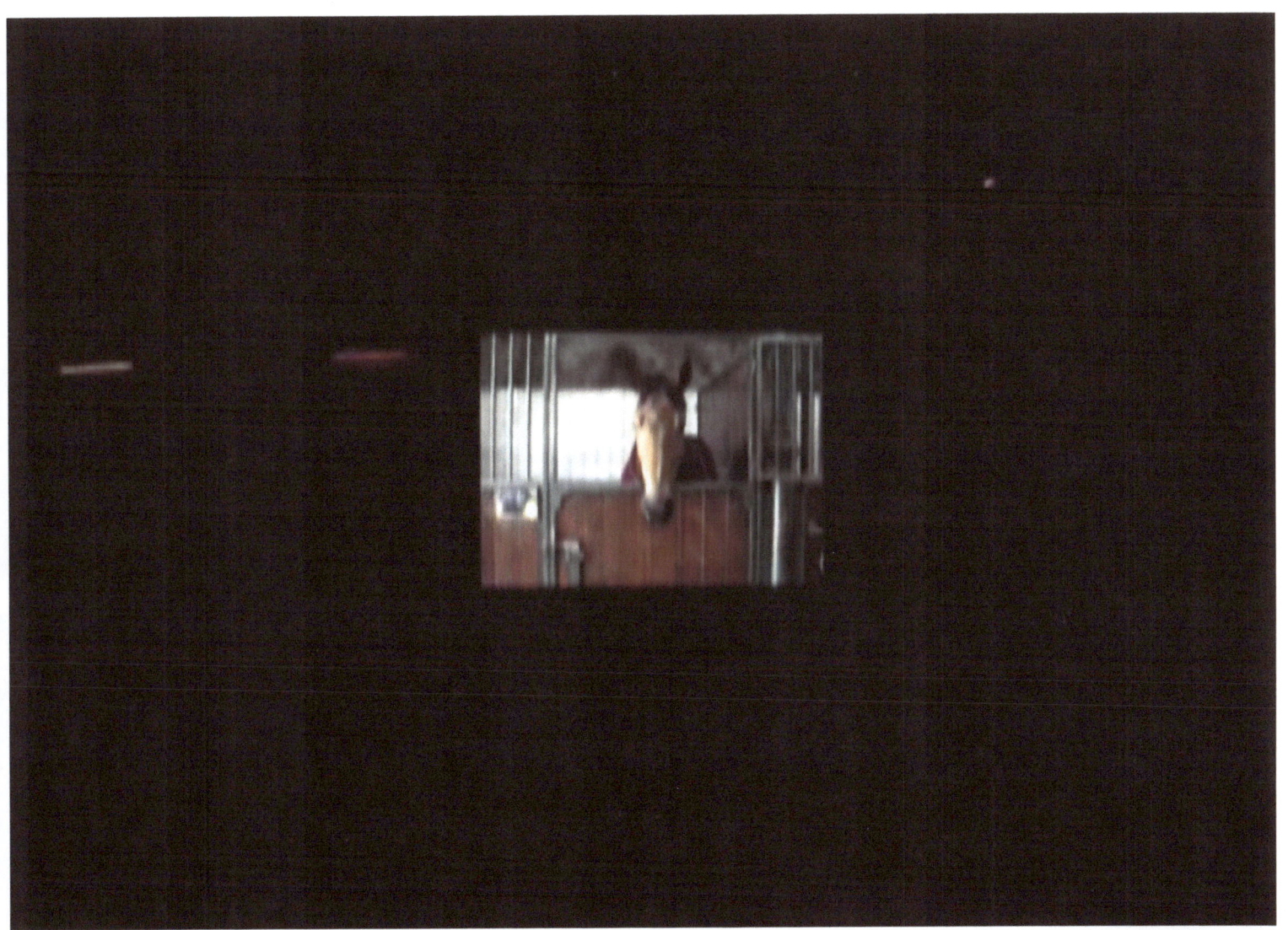

Over the Rainbow...Somewhere

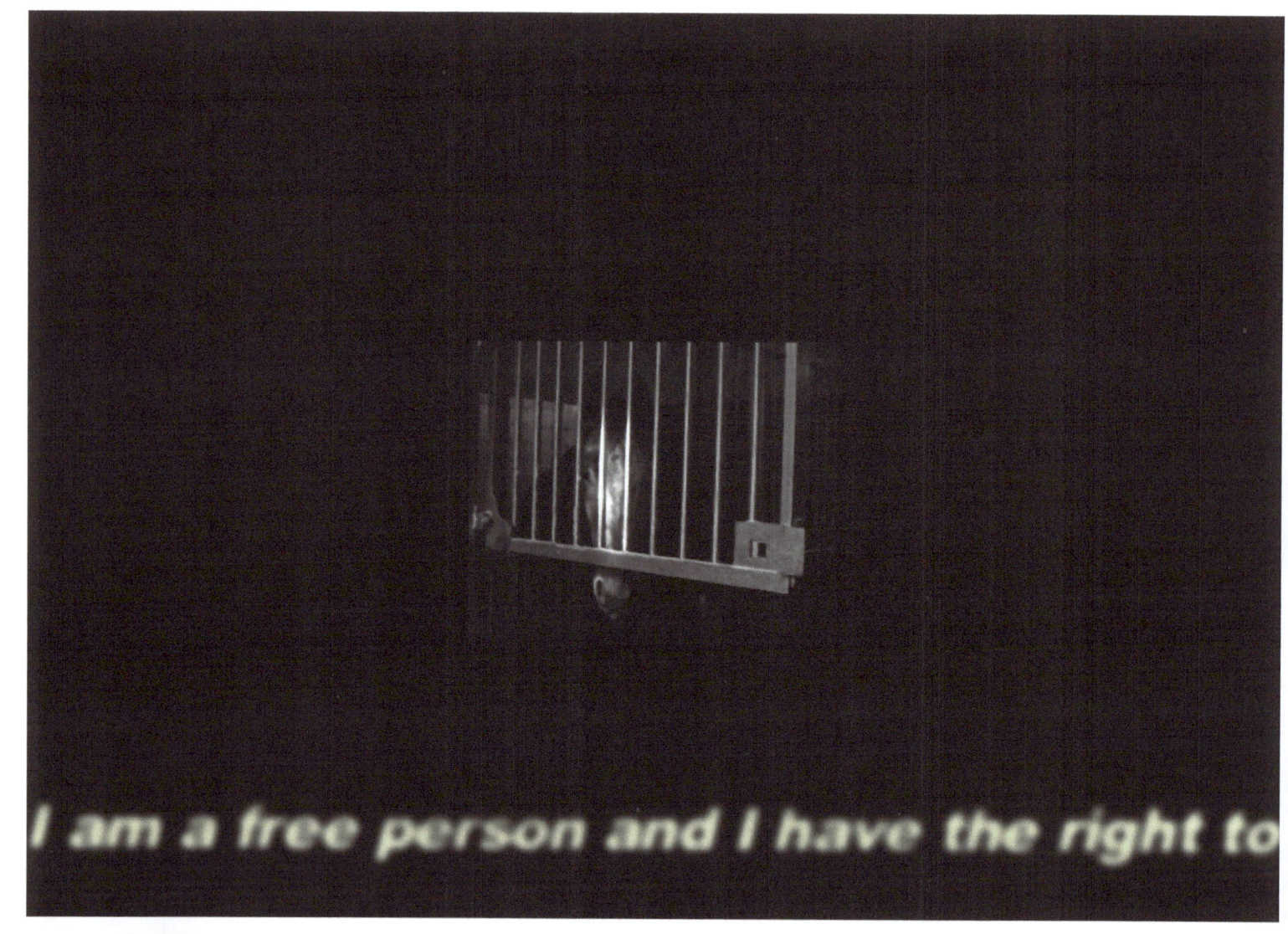

I am a free person and I have the right to

Theatre of Truth(s)

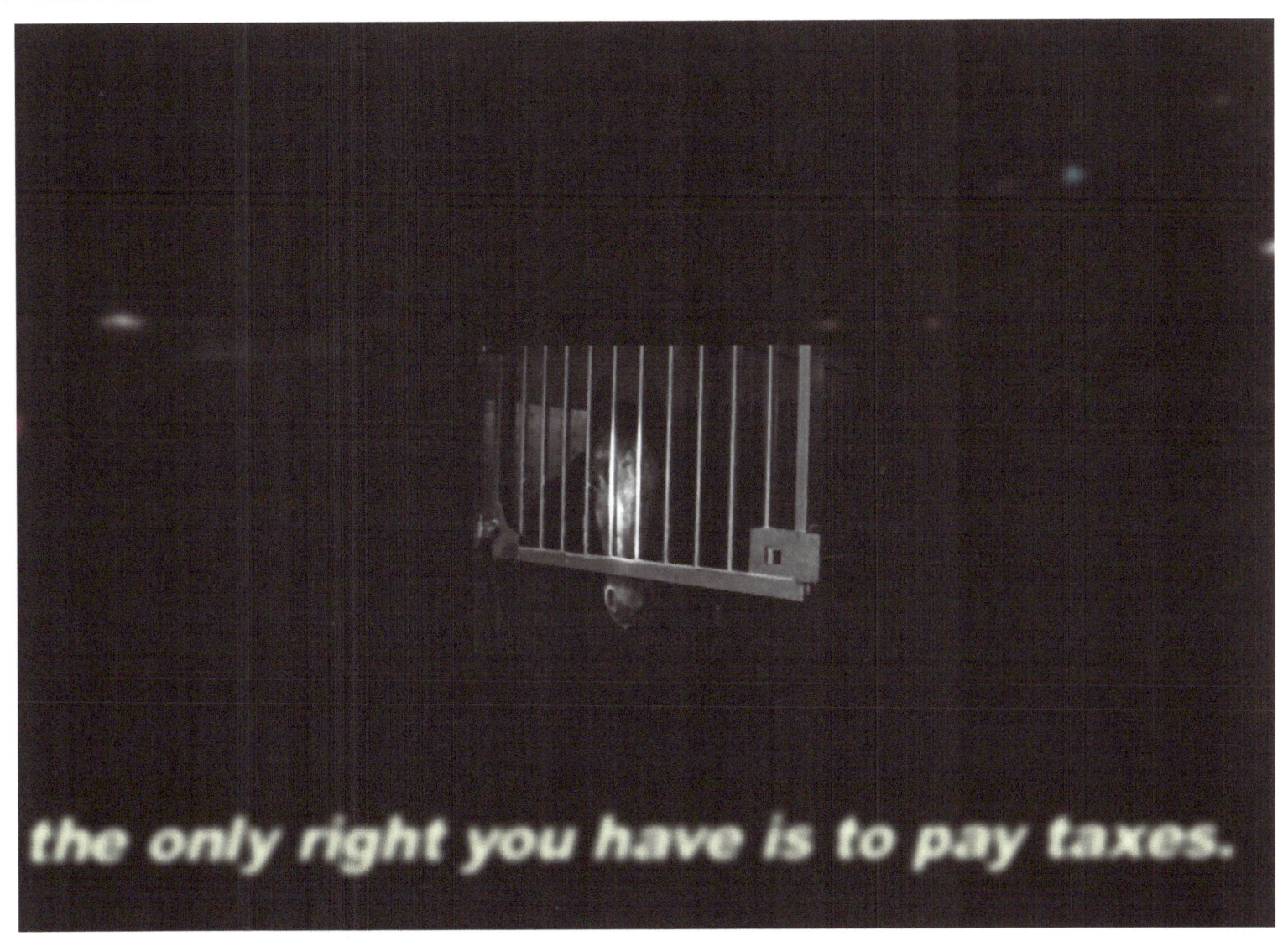

the only right you have is to pay taxes.

Over the Rainbow...Somewhere

47

48

Bumpy Road

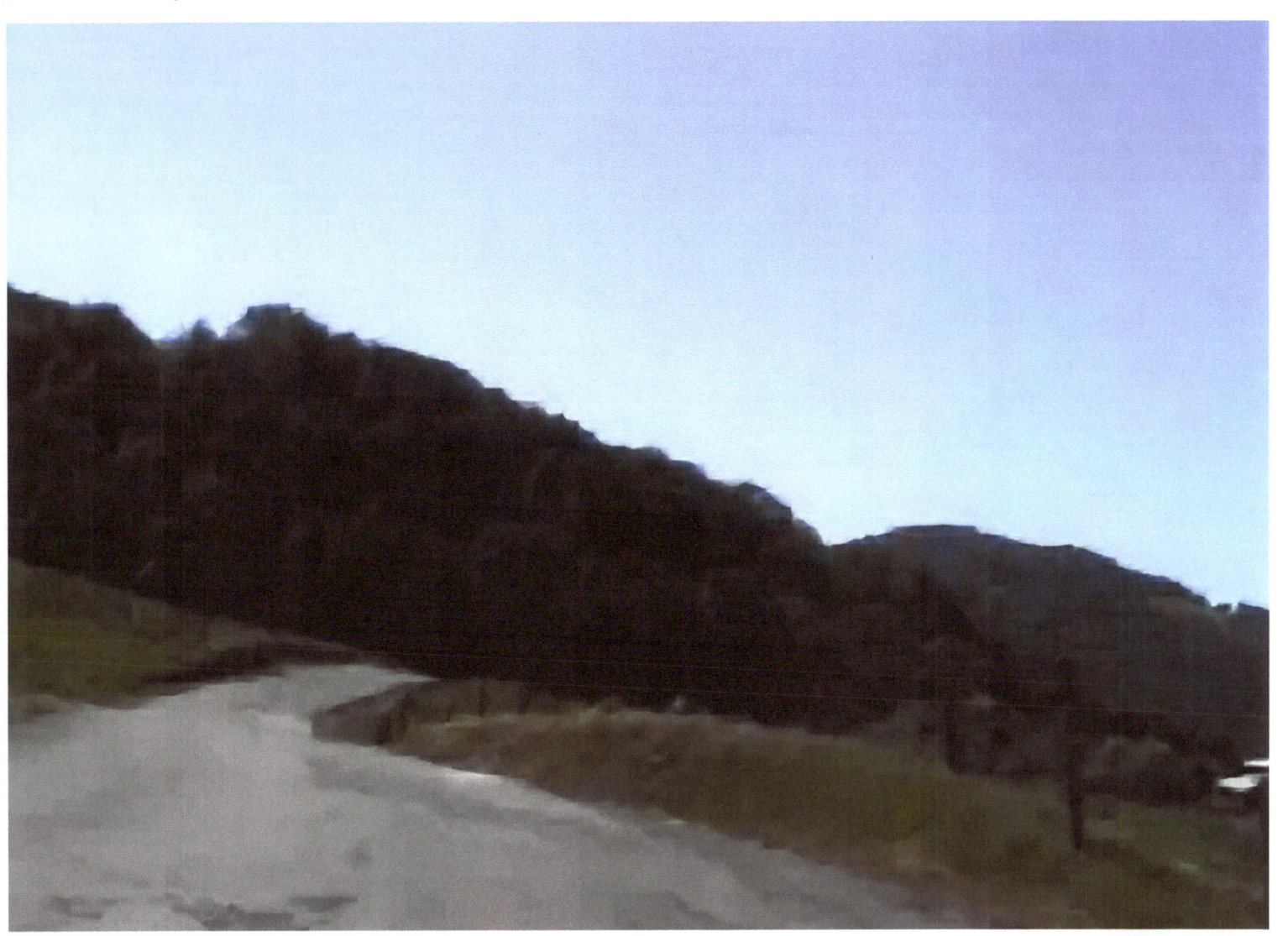

Bumpy Road

49

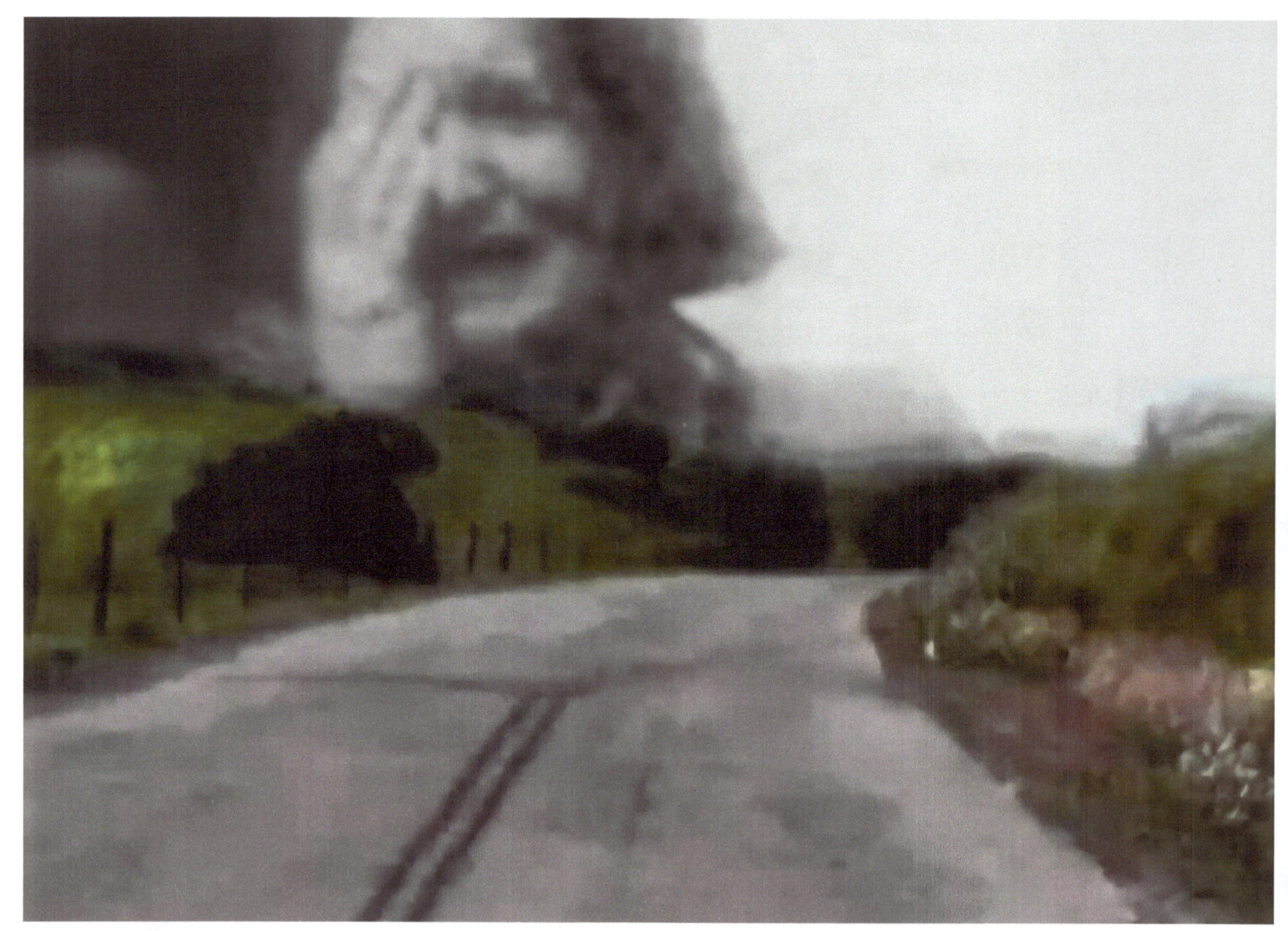

Theatre of Truth(s)

50

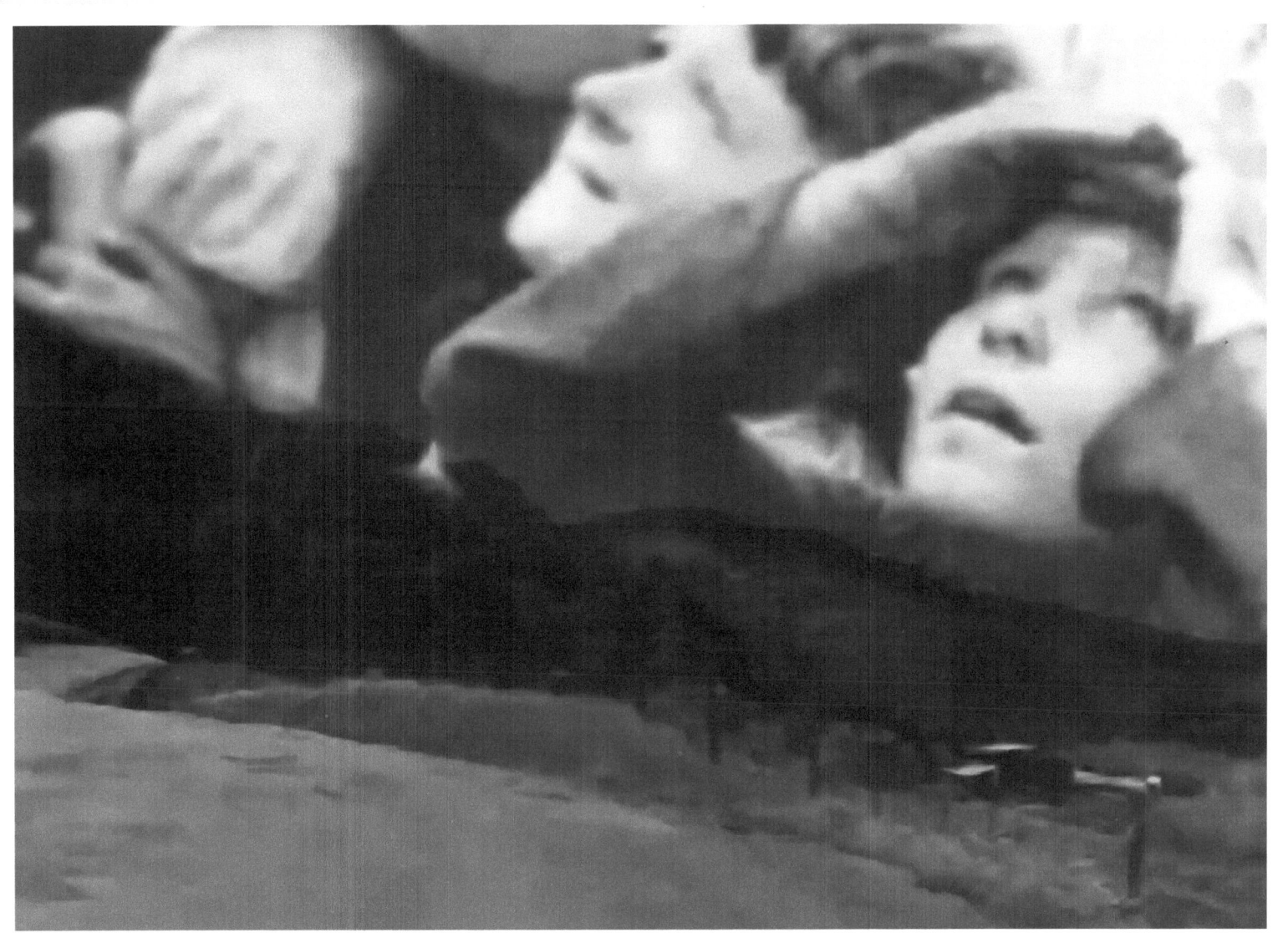

Bumpy Road

51

52

Bogged Down

*P*erformance-based Video Installation.

Bogged Down

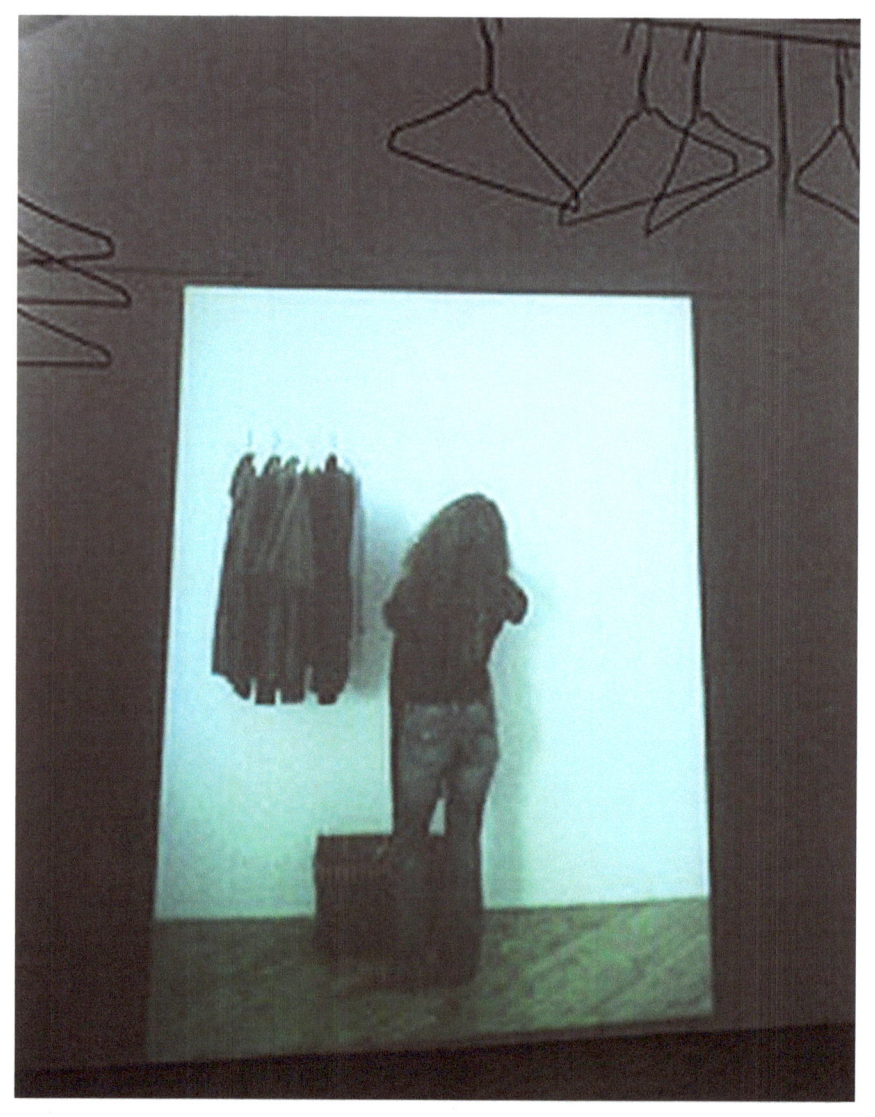

Theatre of Truth(s)

54

I live as sheltered a life as possible. I go

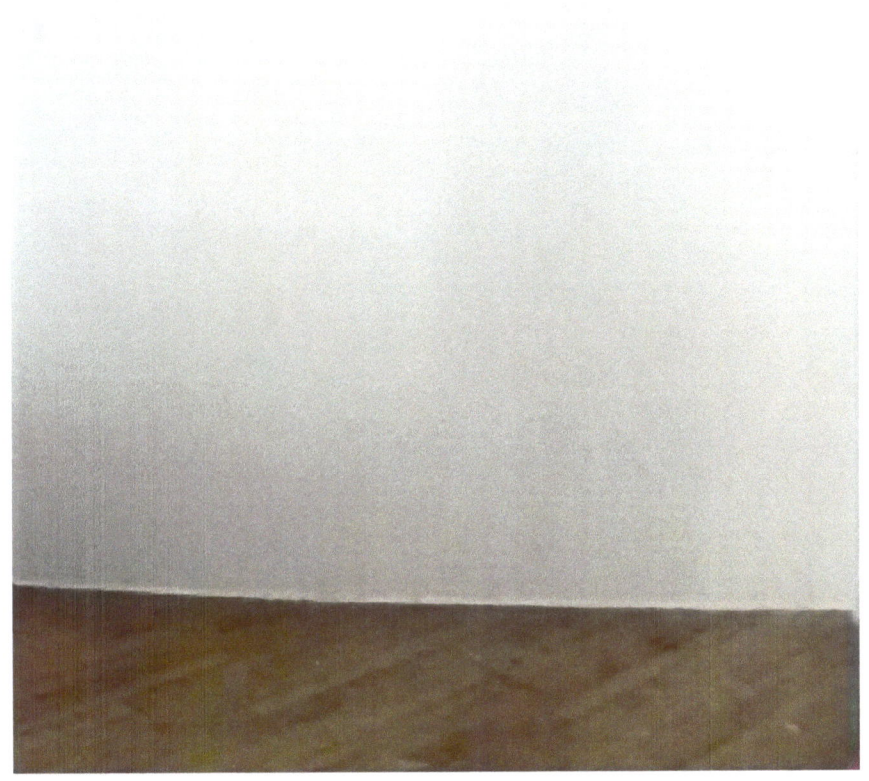

Bogged Down

55

Theatre of Truth(s)

Euphoria
or One Piece Always Missing

Performance-based Video. Video Stills. Art Prints.

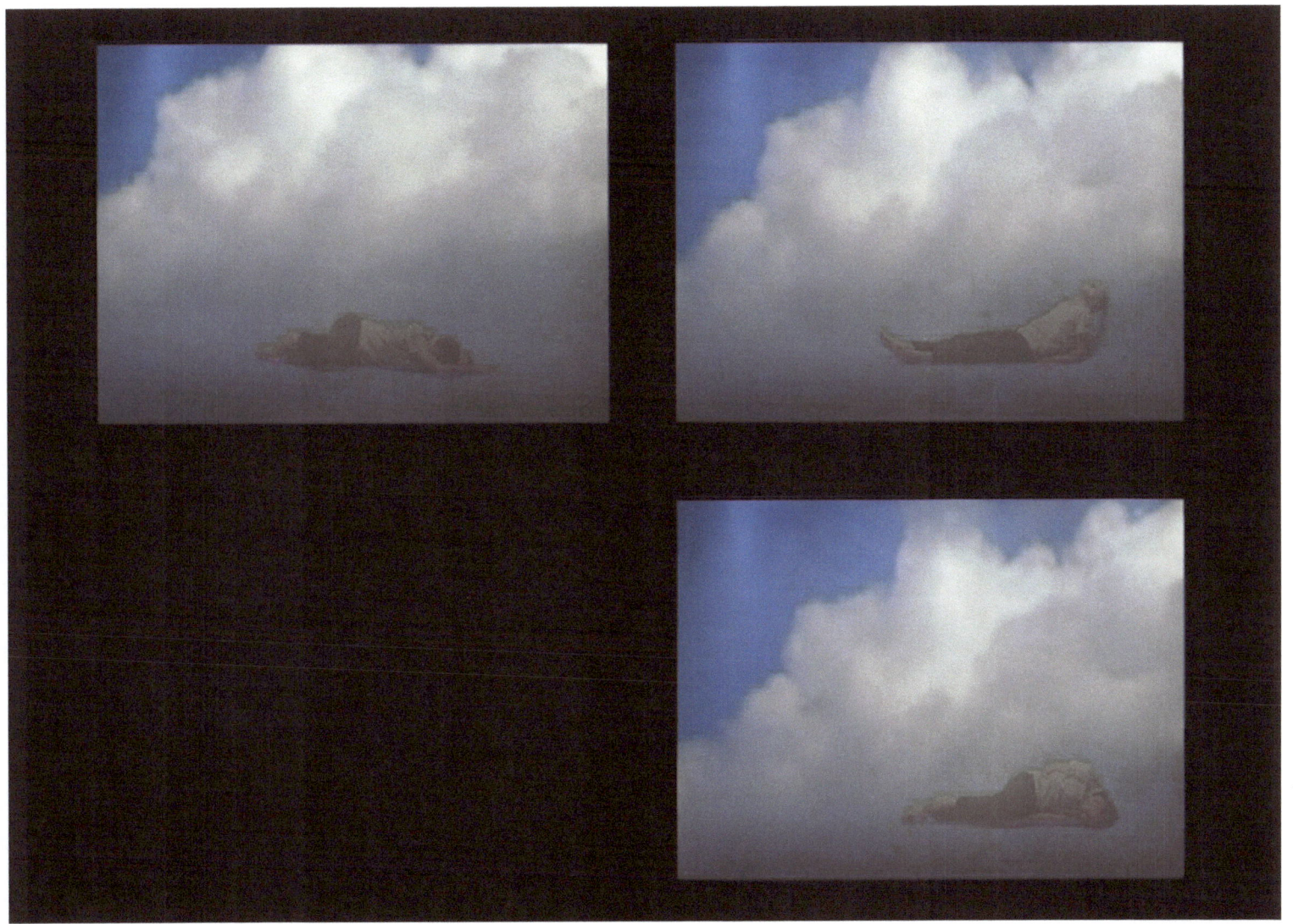

Euphoria or One Piece Always Missing

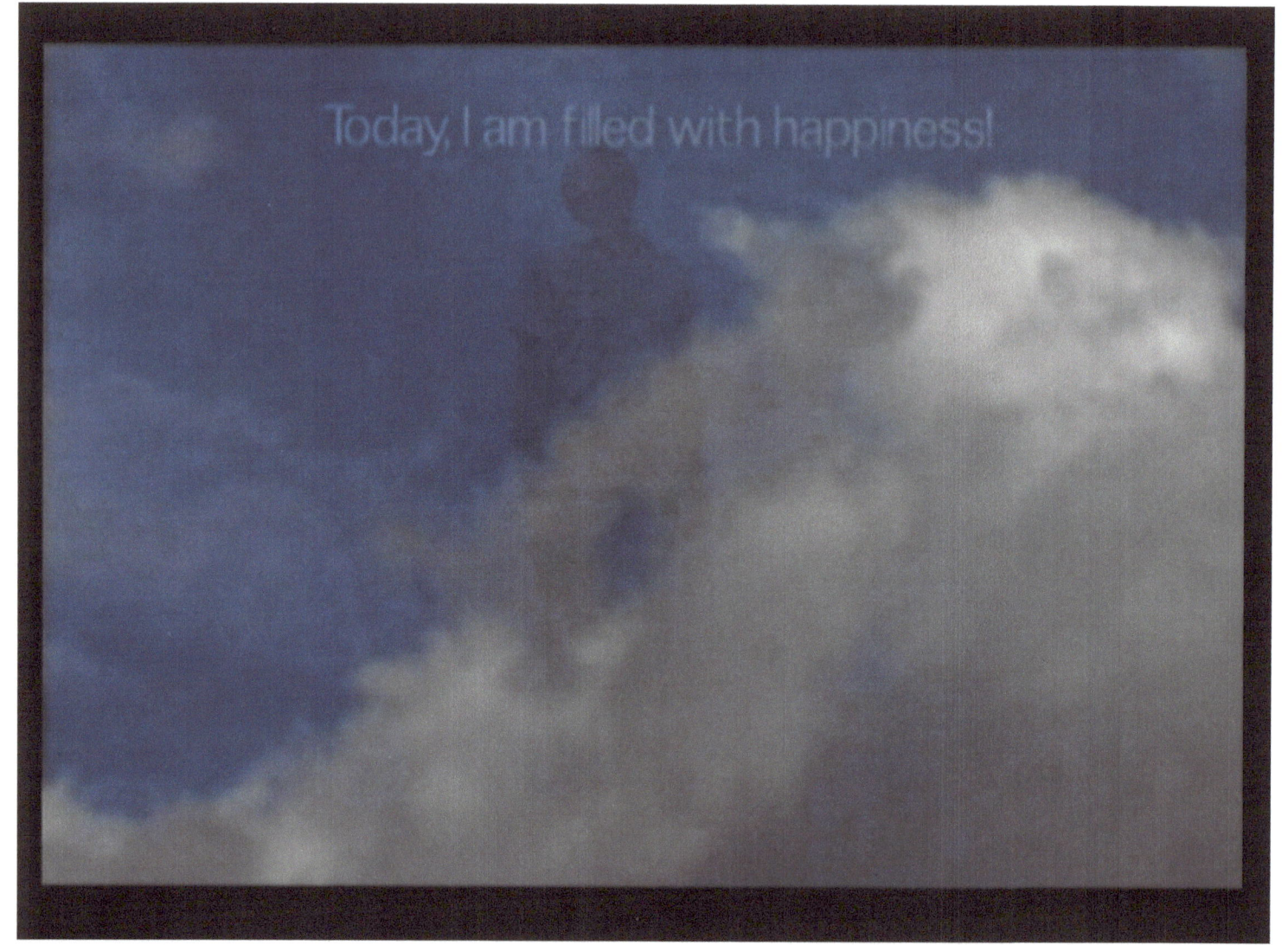

Theatre of Truth(s)

58

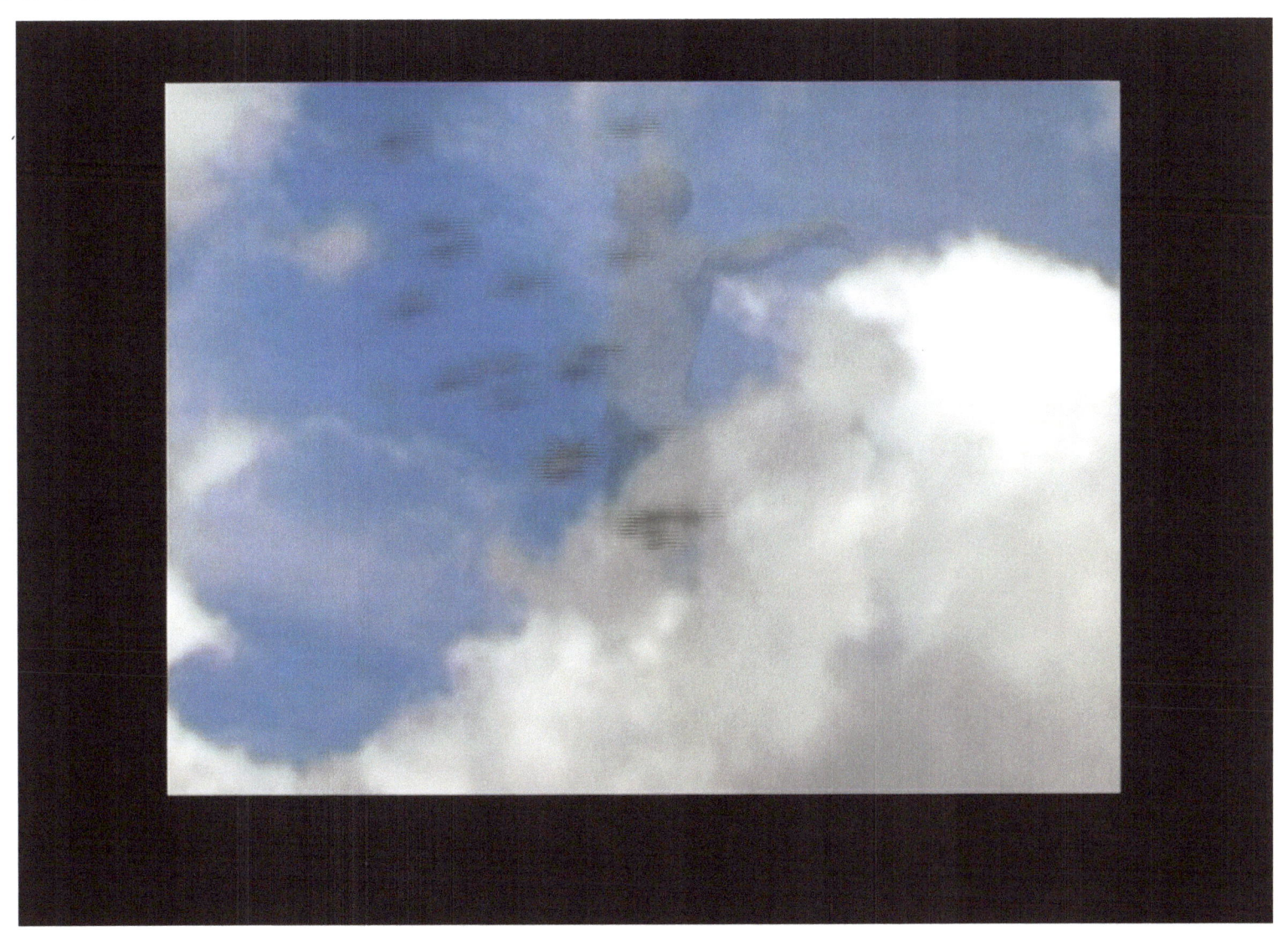

Euphoria or One Piece Always Missing

59

60

Sureseeker in Venice

*V*ideo. Video Stills. Art Prints.

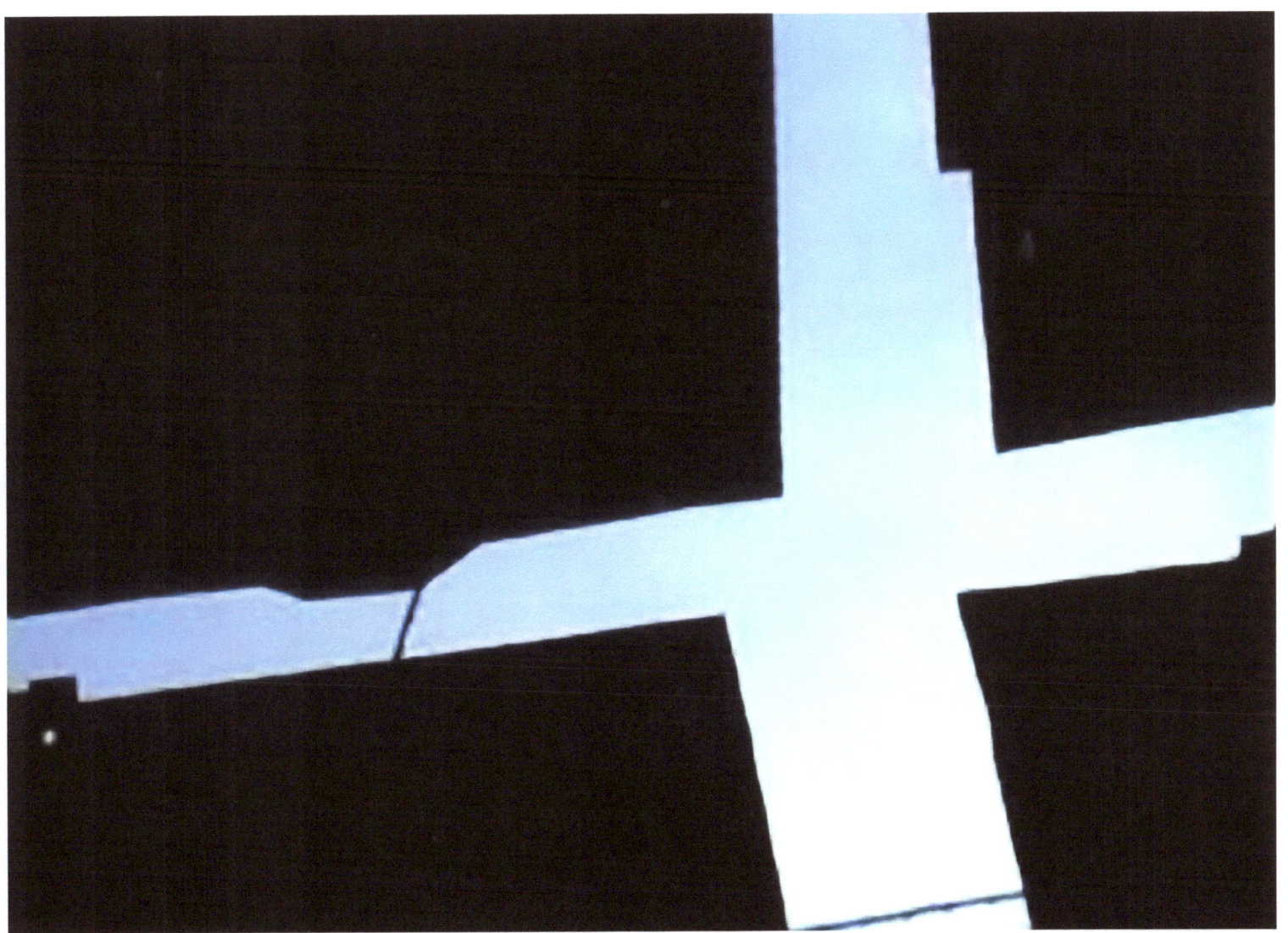

Sureseeker in Venice

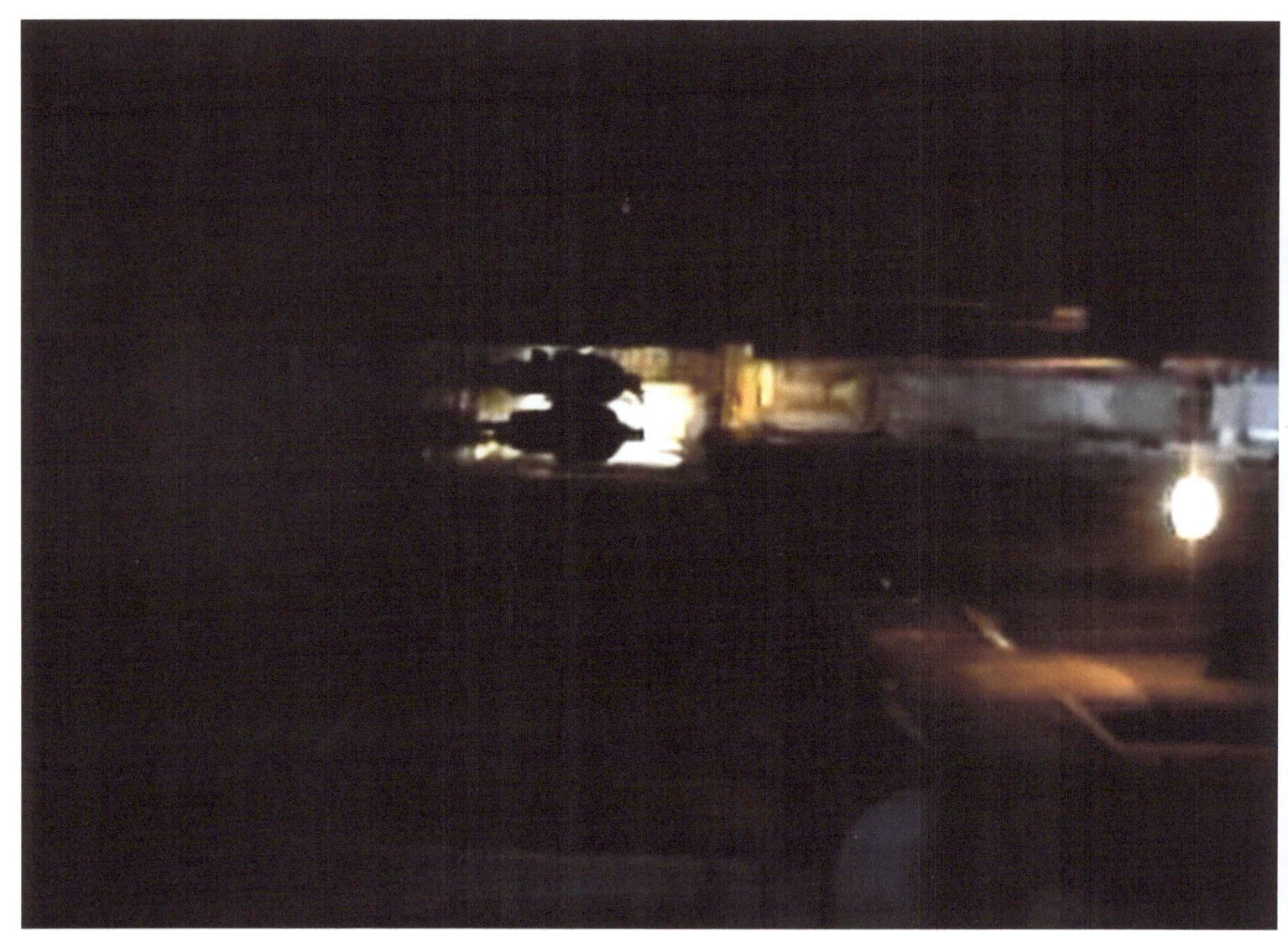

Theatre of Truth(s)

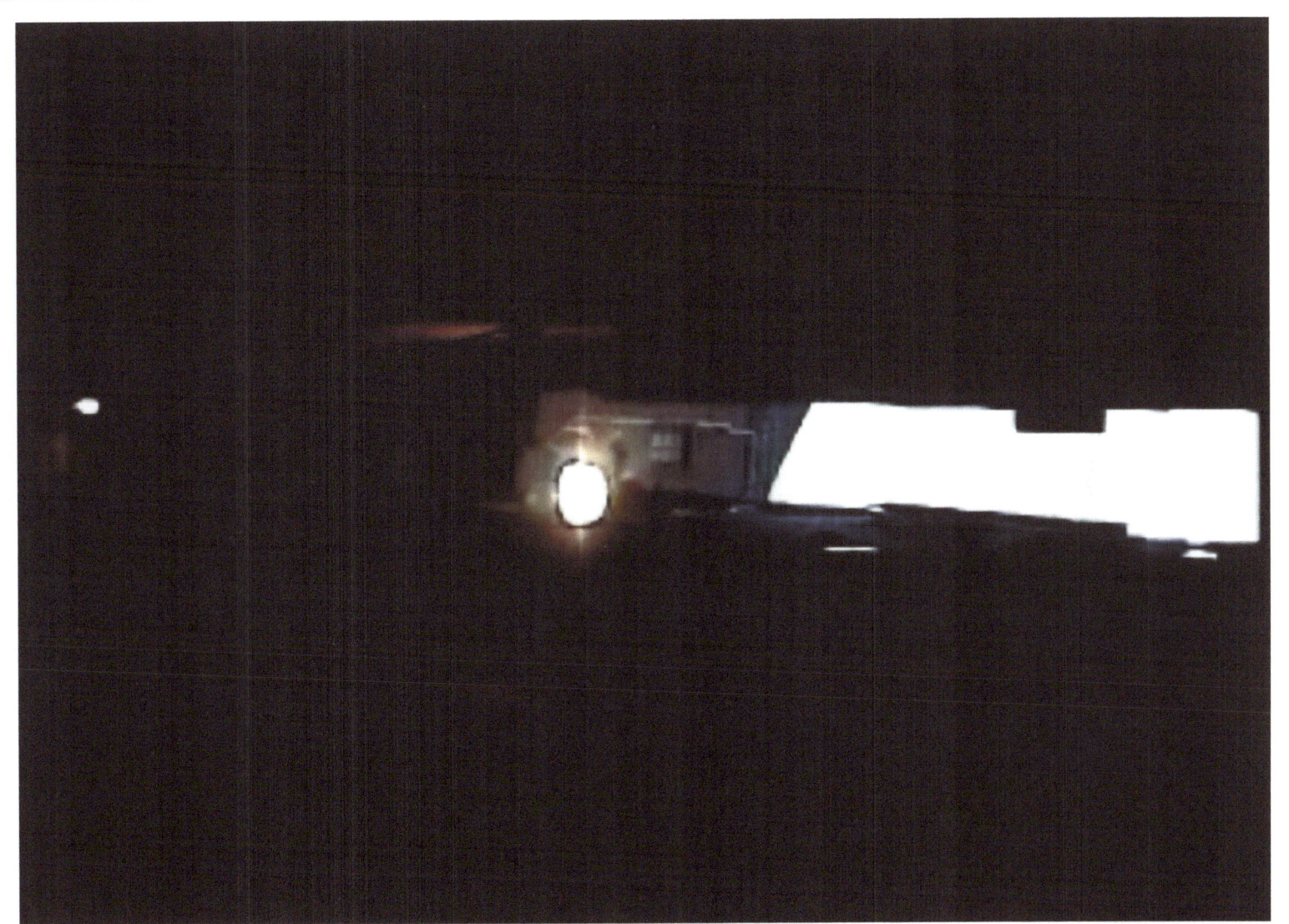

Sureseeker in Venice

63

Theatre of Truth(s)

Inertia

Performance-based Installation. Site Specific.

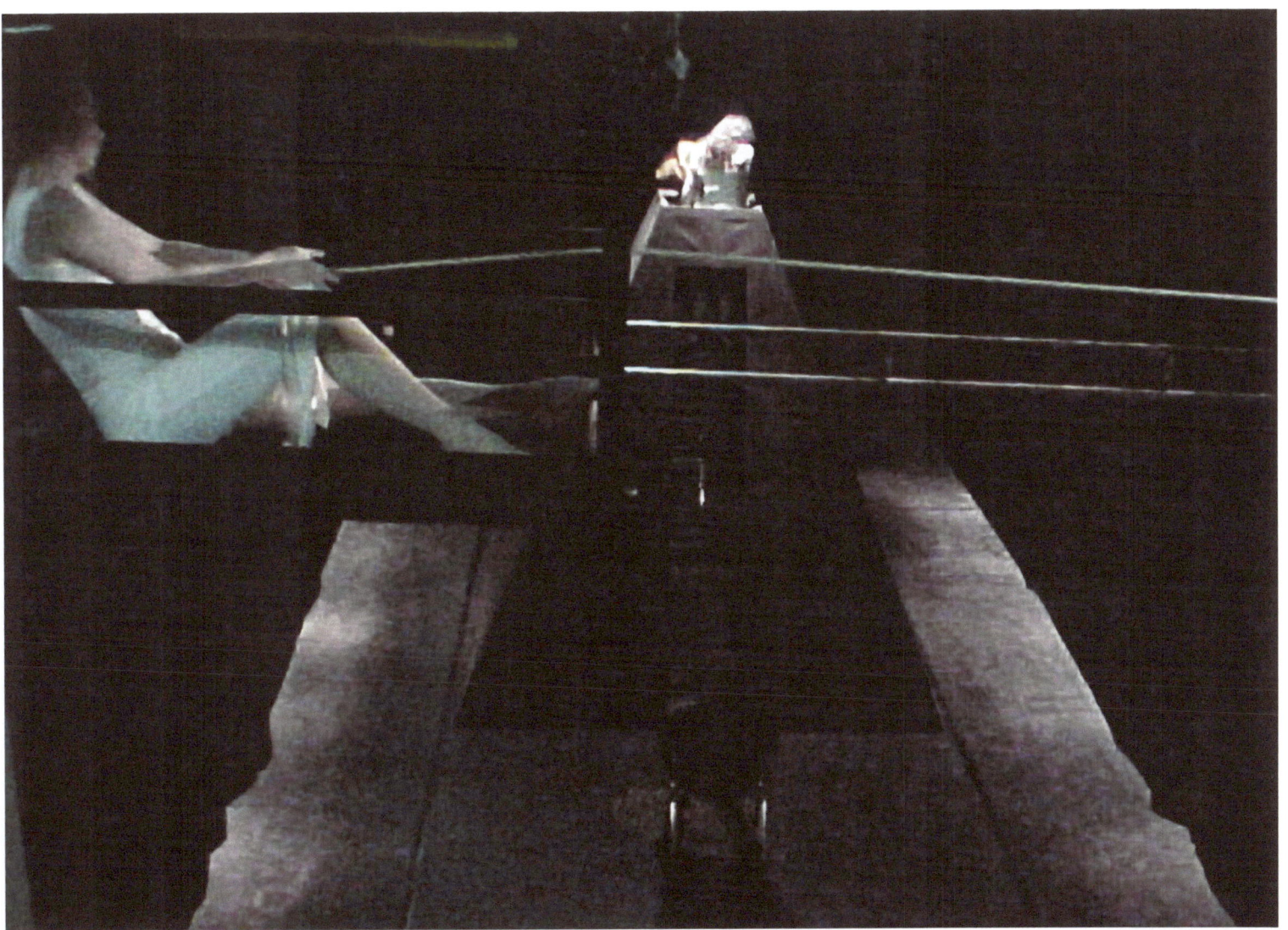

Inertia

65

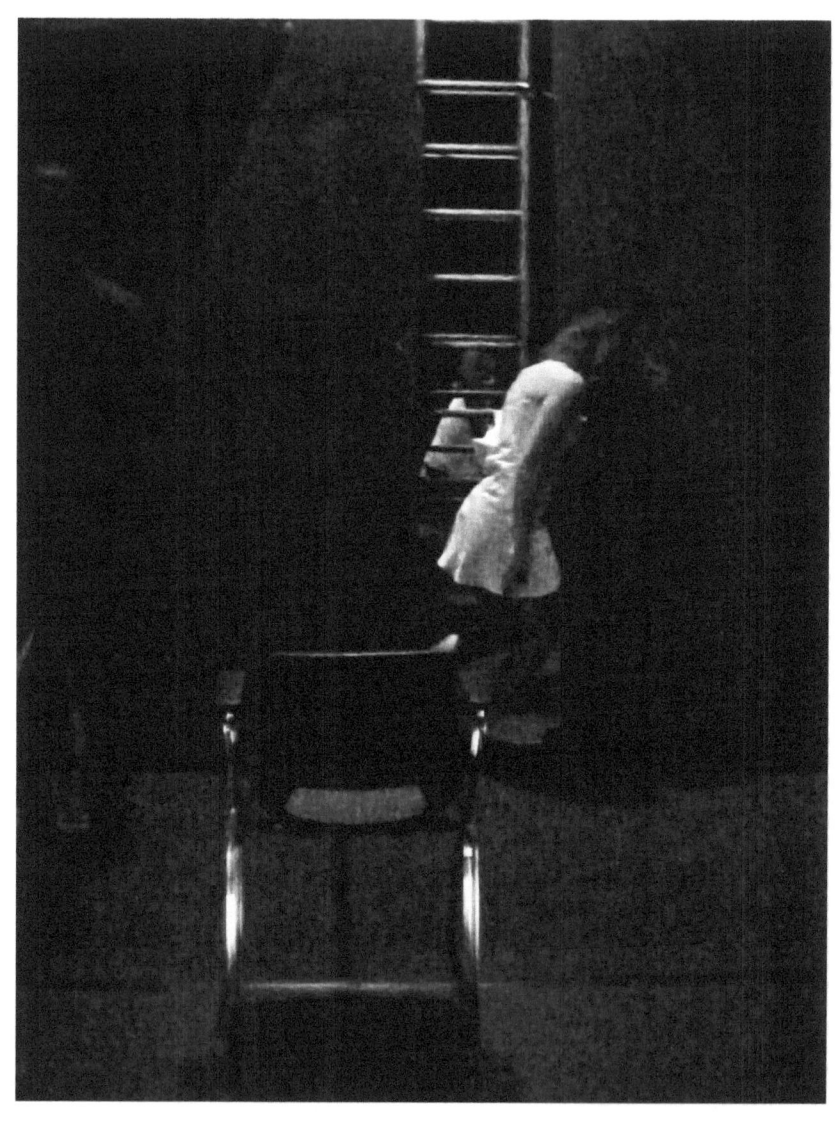

Theatre of Truth(s)

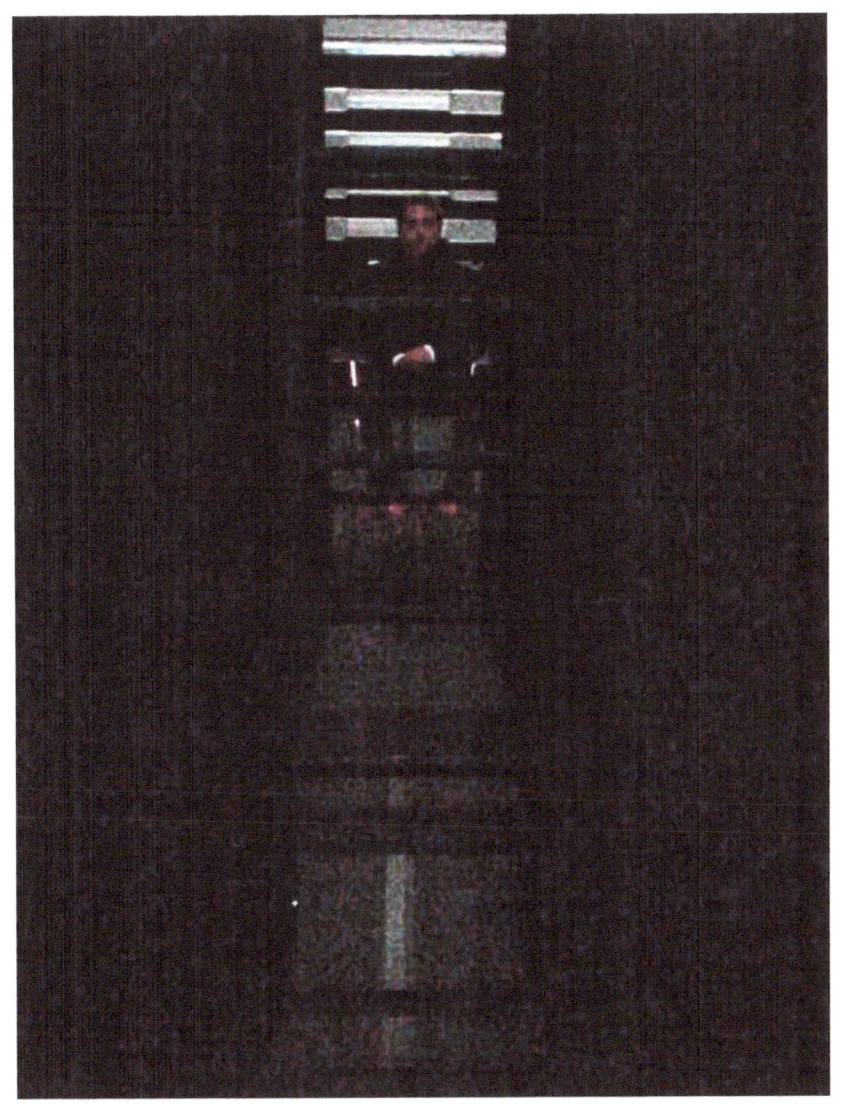

Inertia

67

68

Chestnut

*P*erformance-based Video. Video Stills. Art Prints.

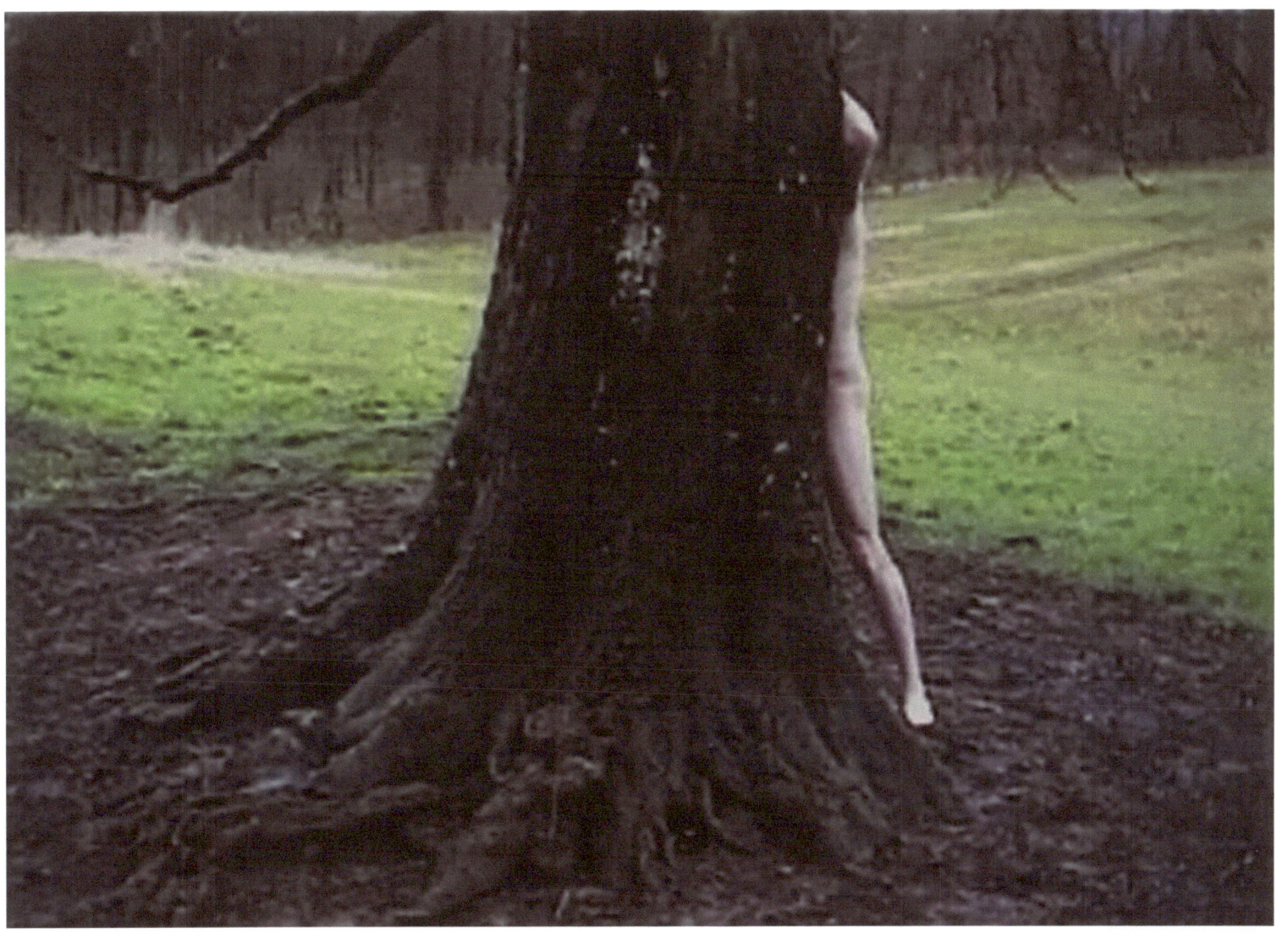

Chestnut

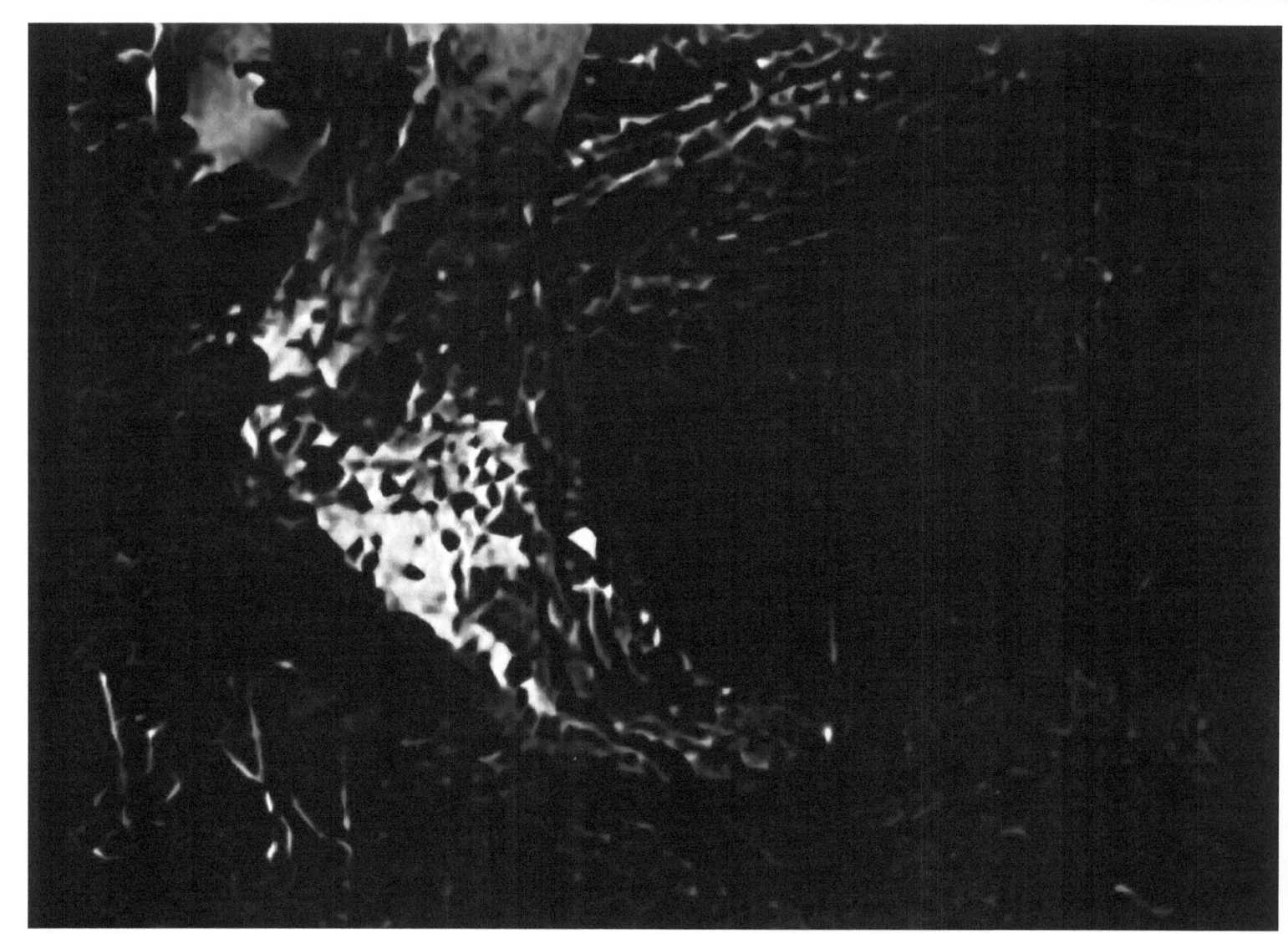

Theatre of Truth(s)

70

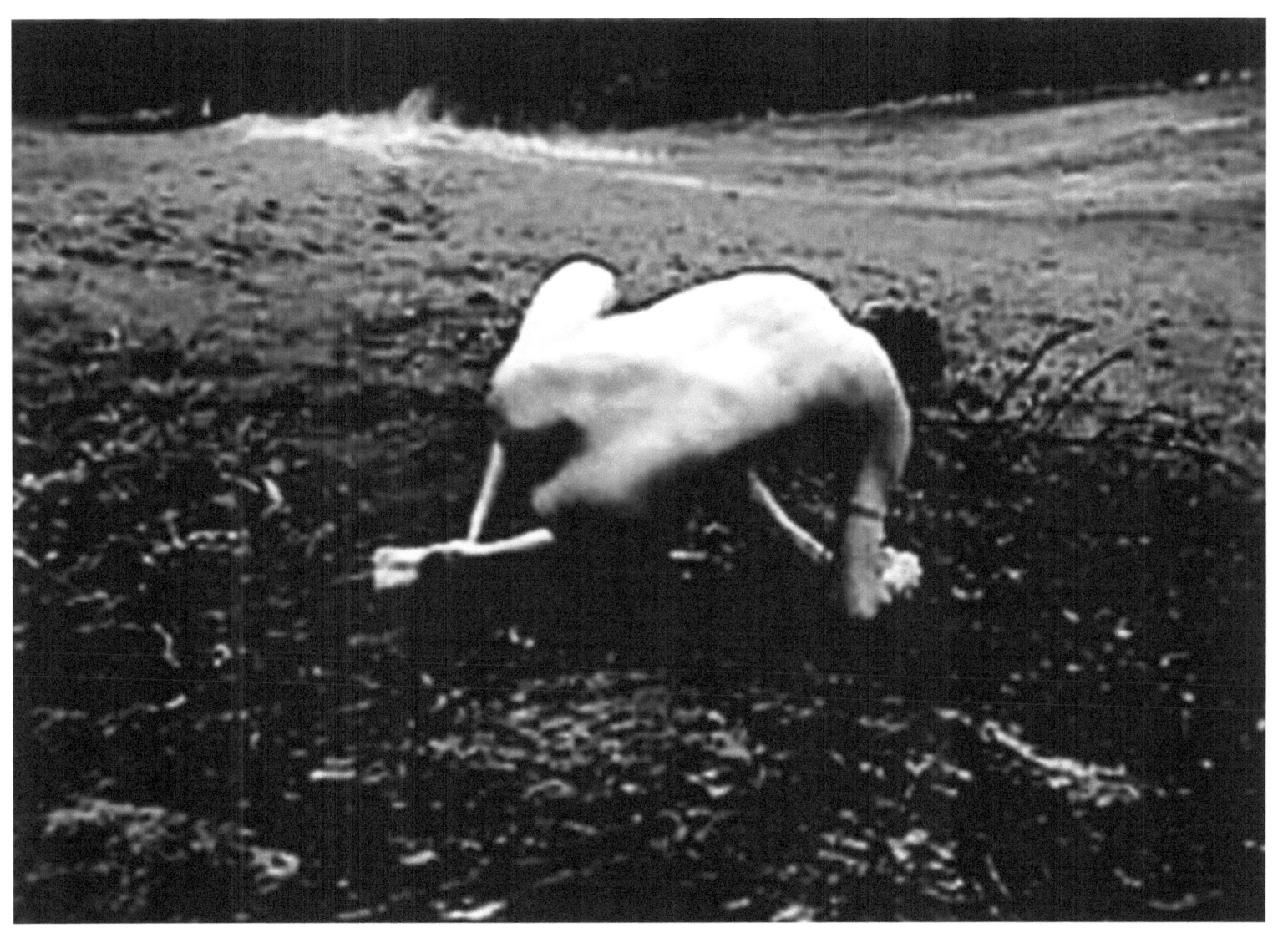

Chestnut

71

72

Performance.

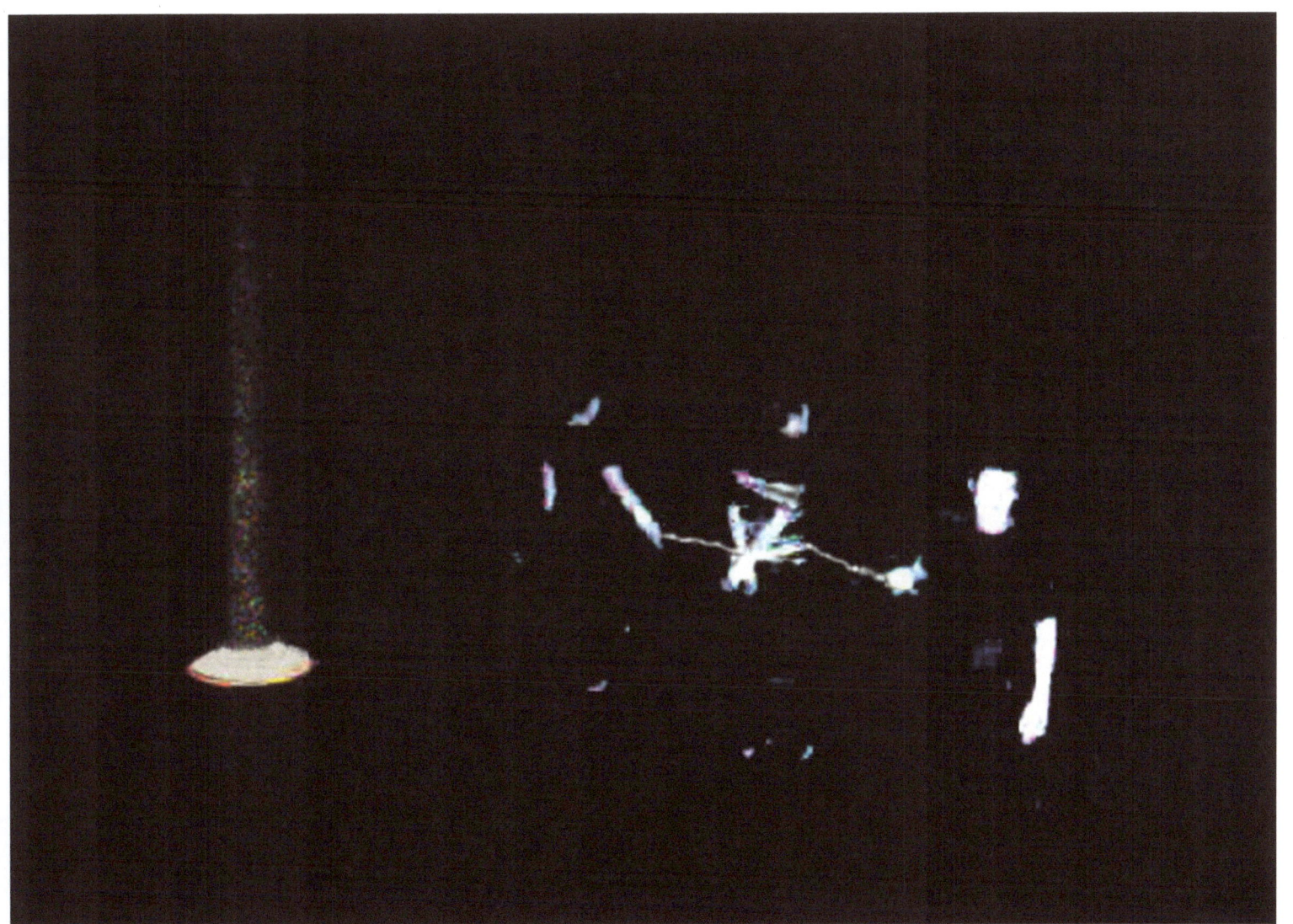

E-Motion

74

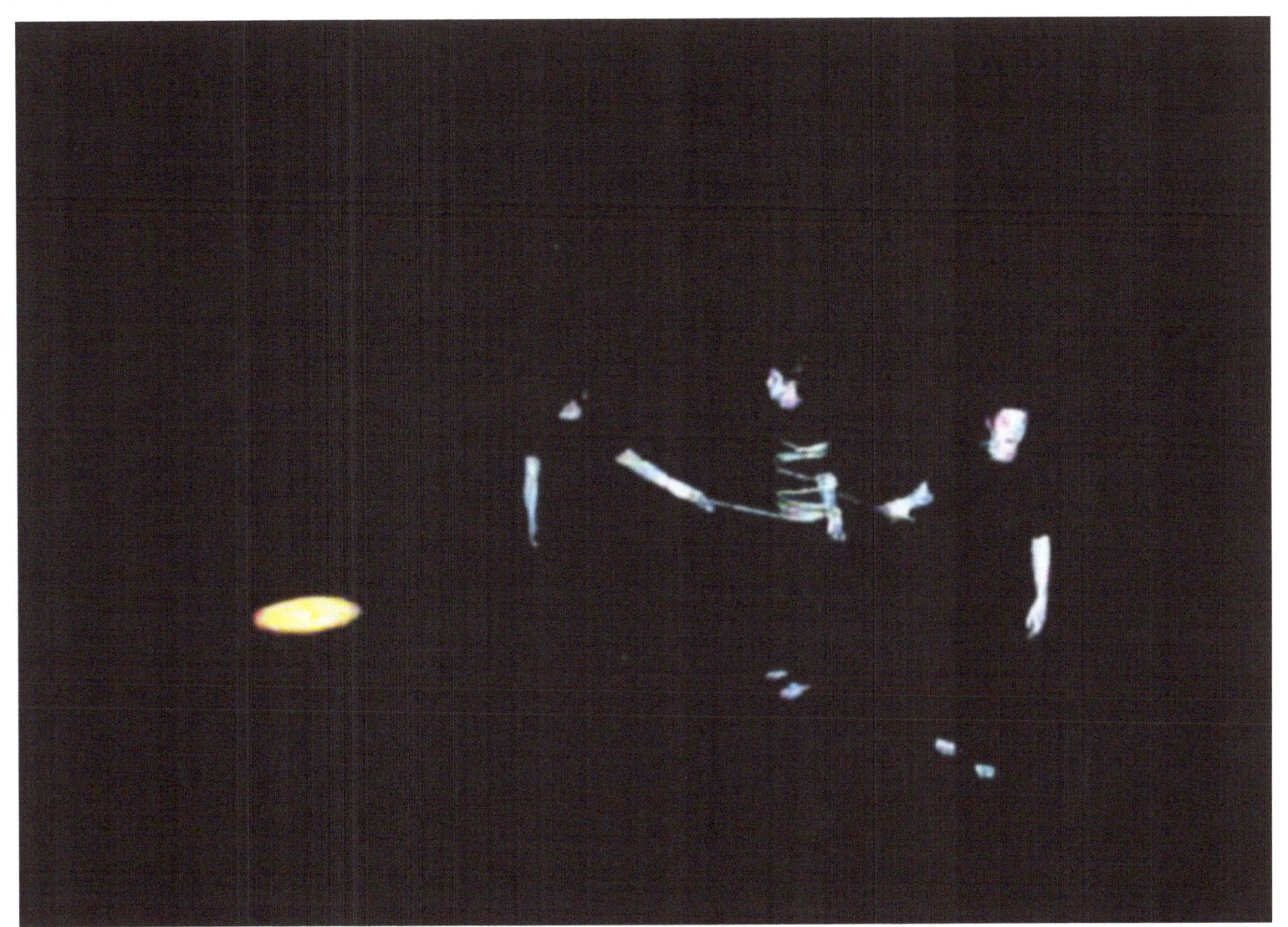

E-Motion

76

Responses

Capturing the ephemeral in one's art has become easier with the help of technology, yet, it continues to challenge makers of such forms. The inverse to "a picture is worth a thousand words," holds true here as there is much value to words when conveying beyond what one sees. Thus, I finish the catalogue with a collage of written impressions, presented on their own, without the juxtaposition of image. The impressions are accurately reproduced although some people preferred to leave their notes anonymous. They are presented in no chronological order and most of times there is no reference to the work described. Each impression tells its own story, which in turn becomes *the work of art*. Naturally, the following pages belong, and are dedicated, to the viewer.

For me, Ella's works are silent poetry that gives very clear elements, which make you feel and think.

(Margarita Stavraki, Greece)

I checked out Ella Joseph's one-night-only installation, "Within Boundary or A Ride in the Air," in her small studio/gallery space on Linwood Avenue. The installation consisted of several IV bags hung from the ceiling by fishing wire, each one containing a swimming fish. Also dangling from the ceiling were headphones, which viewers could put on to hear a sort of ethereal soundscape while they watched a projection of two human legs walking over an abstract background. I'm not sure whether Joseph pulls from dreams to create her work, but this piece was full of the odd little juxtapositions that seem to happen only in dream states. You could speculate endlessly about the meaning of fish swimming around in IV drip bags, or the meaning of the soundscape and the wandering figure. But to me the scene registered as the assured recreation of a strange, subconscious moment not meant to be dissected for meaning. It was like a dream rendered real -- and, like most dreams, it contained elements both of strange grace and vague danger.

(Colin Dabkowski, Buffalo News)

Loved it. It was something I kept thinking about over the weekend. It had great depth. I look forward to seeing more!

(Anonymous)

Your work invites wondering. I love that. Weather in a frame or suspended in space, there is always an invitation to more into your work. Thank you for the journey.

(Priscilla Bowen, Buffalo, NY)

Felt like I was in the Garden of Eden until I got bit by a serpent. A truly nihilistic commentary on main stream society.

(Anonymous)

The Piece "Within Boundary or A Ride in the Air" is the essence of simplicity: projected video of parts of a body in an abstracted landscape, very school-of-Bill-Viola. What makes it most interesting to me is not the image or the accompanying soundtrack, but the way these elements are presented: headphones dangle from the ceiling, alongside IV drip bags, each containing a single live fish. It's a simple, very arresting image, and while I'm not entirely sure what it means in the strictest sense, I can definetely identify the feelings it evokes in me, from initial amazement to mild creepiness to admiration for its elegance.

(Ron Ehmke, Buffalo Infringement Festival Blog)

The audio set up was so unique plus truly made you unware of others - a truly solitary experience - the best audio piece I have been to.

(Lara, Buffalo, NY)

Responses

79

Anticipation is literally hanging in the air at Indigo Gallery, where a unique interactive exhibition that's been up for the past few weeks is slated to have its closing event from 7 to 9 tonight. Ella Joseph's "Awaiting Your Arrival" explores feelings of waiting something (or someone) through a combination of hanging objects, video and photography. During the exhibition's opening on feb. 4, Joseph filmed those who attended. During tonight's closing, photographs taken from those videos will be on view, allowing a kind of full-circle exploration of what it means to expect and be expected.

(Colin Dabkowski, Buffalo News)

Very compelling ways of creating borders and liminal experiences. The visitors are the art but they are separated from the art...brilliant!

(Anonymous)

A unique experience enticed the thought of forced group opinion by way of mass news outlets underlined by childhood wholesome nostalgic song.

(Anonymous)

[...] whimsical, slightly unsettling, partially edible art installation.

(Colin Dabkowski)

I always find a celestial feel with your work. "Awaiting Your Arrival" had just that. Dreamy, etheric, beautiful.

(Sue Royce, Buffalo, NY)

I was memerized by the circular moevement of the tied bodies and sad when the sand stopped falling.

(Anonymous)

When we first went into the exhibition we didn't use the headphones and I felt as though I was looking at the world through a cloud from above. I was enjoying the fluff of cotton candy and feeling young and carefree again. It was a happy feeling...When I went back in and used the headphones I listened to the world as it is, with the clouds and floaty feeling ripped away. I was closed in, riveted to what I was hearing, with the rest of the world closing in and at disparity to the cotton candy world.

(Sunny Mathews, Niagara Falls, NY)

Waiting outside in the busy cafe was by no means preparation for entrance into the space. As I came around the corner the black volume engulfed me and I moved slowly towards the strange pyramid in the center. The others were there too and we as the observers suddenly became a part of the space [...]. After leaving I felt changed, I felt it was possible for my body to slow down [...].

(Jennifer LeMasters, USA)

It was something new to me. I didn't quite understand it. I was suffocated in trying to see what was happening and paralyzed by the too many people around me.

(Raluca Dumitrescu, Romania)

Responses

81

I am always stimulated by your work - I see new things every time I see it and I love the concept that I bring something to the art and in so doing, become part of the art itself. An obvious concept that your work and theory has brought home to me. That being said I find it a little scary that the hanging IV bags become a woman hanging and your image, laying on the ground, was a crushed up cigarette for me. Never to be seen again!

(Ginny Sundell, Buffalo, NY)

I was very impressed by several elements that brought me into the state of inertia. I didnt know your title until I saw it written in the flyer. Then, I could understand why my body was exhausted.

(Clara Cot, Spain)

Being there for 20 minutes, I recognized that I got more nervous and restless; there were too many people to reach a meditative state, which I thought I was supposed to get into with such artwork. When I recognized my own impatience and the almost aggressive atmosphere in the room, I understood that the audience is part of the installation and we are not supposed to just watch an object but to observe the progress in our mind during the time of the performance. From that point, I was much more focused on the interaction between the artwork and the audience rather than just trying to detect meaning of the images and the artwork itself.

(Daniel Kaminski, Germany)

Your work has some elements that remind me of the Happenings in the Sixties. I also found similarities with one movie from that period, "Last Year in Marienbad." The way you deal with time brought me to those images I used to love.

(Joan Munne, Spain)

Elements...the canes from awaiting arrival...the fish from Jonah...lifesize cutout of Ella here, real Ella in the next room, moving images on the screen, laughter in the next room....everything evocative, ressurecting memories in my mind, experiences...everything a flowing interconnected piece.

(Anonymous)

I love your idea that one work generates another. Each piece becomes a part of you and in turn a part of every new piece. "One form generates another" is the perfect way to describe the infinite narrative.

(Paul Rehac, Buffalo, NY)

I love the "yin-yang" of your work. There are so many people who go through life without seeing what can be beautiful and meaningful in the "darker" aspects of life; they choose to ignore and not learn because they are afraid. I used to be one of those people who was never interested in exploring the darker aspects of life, but I believe those experiences make us stronger and more sensitive. I hope you are able to keep us thinking and evolving for a long time.

(Jacki, Buffalo, NY)

Responses

83